SpringerBriefs in Economics

More information about this series at http://www.springer.com/series/8876

Niklas Arvidsson

Building a Cashless Society

The Swedish Route to the Future of Cash Payments

 Springer

OPEN

Niklas Arvidsson
Royal Institute of Technology
Stockholm, Sweden

ISSN 2191-5504   ISSN 2191-5512   (electronic)
SpringerBriefs in Economics
ISBN 978-3-030-10688-1   ISBN 978-3-030-10689-8   (eBook)
https://doi.org/10.1007/978-3-030-10689-8

Library of Congress Control Number: 2018966535

This Springer imprint is published by the registered company Springer Nature Switzerland AG
The registered company address is: Gewerbestrasse 11, 6330 Cham, Switzerland

Preface

The last decade has shown a decrease in the use of cash in Sweden, and this is likely to continue in the coming years. The value of cash in circulation in Swedish crowns dropped 50% between the peak in 2007 and the low figures of 2018. If we turn our eyes to the future, it may be the case that Sweden is a cashless society in just a few years, perhaps already in 2023 AD.

There are many reasons behind this development including regulation, innovation, technological advancements, trust in the banking system, demographics, lobbying and campaigns both by those wanting to reduce the uses of cash and by those who want to keep cash, consumer behavior, and more.

A majority of Swedes seem to like this development while some groups do not. Elderly, people with physical and/or cognitive disabilities, immigrants, and small retailers in rural areas are dependent on cash and are not always favoring this development.

No matter which viewpoint you have regarding the future of cash, it is without doubt we live in interesting times when we talk about money and payments! And, this book aims to provide greater insight into this transformation of our economies.

Stockholm, Sweden   Niklas Arvidsson

Acknowledgements

This book could not have been written without the valuable work with colleagues as well as the support from organizations during my research endeavors. I am greatly indebted to Jonas Hedman at Copenhagen Business School and Björn Segendorf at the the Riksbank of Sweden with whom I pursued the study of retailers in Sweden but also have done several different research projects with. Also to Jan Markendahl at the Royal Institute of Technology who has been a research companion in the area of technologies and payments for the last decade. Bengt Nilervall and the Swedish Trade Federation have not only provided access to Swedish retailers but also been an insightful source of information and knowledge in the area of payments. Many different persons in the Swedish Bankers' Association, in Card Payments Sweden, as well as in Swedish banks have been important sources of both information and knowledge during my years as a researcher. And there are many persons and companies in the innovative Fintech industry in Sweden that has provided knowledge as well as novel ideas related to payments that should be acknowledged. None mentioned, all remembered.

Special thanks are given to the organizations and people that allowed me to interview them when writing this book. This includes Jenny Lindroth and Situation Stockholm, Mikael Åsman and Elisabeth Tunberg as well as Svenska Kyrkan in Sundbyberg, Ola Nilsson and PRO, as well as Ylva Lundkvist Fridh and Rural Sweden.

I must also acknowledge all the valuable discussions, seminars, and experiences discussed and shared by my colleagues at the Department of Industrial Economics and Management (INDEK) at the Royal Institute of Technology in Stockholm, Sweden.

In the end, this book is written entirely by me and all potential limitations are entirely my responsibility.

Contents

Chapter 1
Money: The Greatest Innovation in the History of Humanity

The Essence of This Book

Money is a central part of everybody's life and every society and has been more important for humanity than the wheel, the printing press, the steam engine, and the Internet. Money is one of the greatest innovations in our history! I therefore decided to write this book about money.

Not only is money one of the greatest innovations, it is also currently being radically transformed in a way that has not happened in centuries. The last radical or even paradigmatic transformation of money came in the seventeenth century when the Riksbank of Sweden and Bank of England introduced the first money provided by central banks. Yes, we had had money—in the form of shells, stones, rings, coins, bills, or other forms—provided and backed by kings, emperors, and other head of states a long time before this. But this is when money became what it is today, i.e., a guarantee of value provided by a central bank, backed by a state, and issued in the form of bills and coins. What we simply call cash. No matter if we use US dollars, euros, Chinese RMBs, Russian rubles, or Swedish crowns, the basic form was introduced in the seventeenth century and is still an important part of many societies.

We now see, however, that the concept we call cash is challenged! We are actually discussing whether we may see entire economies without cash. The idea of cashless societies is not new, but it has not really been realistic until today as digitalization is reshaping fundamental dimensions of our societies, where money is one of them. And why should not money be transformed? Most things come to an end, and it is likely this may happen to cash as well.

This book explores how a cashless society is developed and look like by studying Sweden. I know that Sweden is not like other countries and that all the insights from understanding Sweden cannot be exported to other countries. This is not my aim. I aim to explain what made Sweden becoming a cashless society, to provide a discussion of challenges and opportunities that lies ahead, and to ignite much needed

© The Author(s) 2019
N. Arvidsson, *Building a Cashless Society*, SpringerBriefs in Economics,
https://doi.org/10.1007/978-3-030-10689-8_1

discussions of how less cash—or even no cash—will transform our economies. Because this is a societal challenge we must learn to master.

This is a book about the abdication of the king formerly known as *Cash*. The projected abdication of *Cash* in Sweden is expected to happen in 2023 AD.

I hope you will enjoy reading this book and that it evokes new thoughts and engaged debates about the future of cash.

Money: The Center of Development Since the Birth of Humanity

Money in some form has probably been at the center of trade and business since the birth of humanity. Unless favors are based entirely on charity or an eternal promise to make good in return, some sort of payment system is needed to stimulate trade and thereby enable specialization and prosperity. Even an economic system entirely based on nonpecuniary trade needs agreements on terms of trade, for instance, how to make a fair trade between rice and milk, which in essence lays the foundation for one important feature of money, i.e., unit of account. If 1 kilo rice can be exchanged for, let's say, 2 liters of milk, the system has set a value on both products and this value can then be accounted for via a monetary system. And such monetary systems have proven to be important for development throughout the history of humanity. I will argue that they are a critical part of the human history and development.

From time to time, there are discussions of what can be said to be the greatest innovation in the history of humanity. There are several potential candidates for this prestigious award, and it is a difficult task to judge this. What should be the yardstick and how do we compare innovations made several thousand years apart? All in all, this is not a fair contest. We will most likely overestimate the value of innovations that are recent since they have had a strong impact on our own lives while underestimating those made in ancient history. Bearing this in mind, I will never-theless make a case for one important innovation: money. I assume this did not come as a great surprise given the topic of the book.

Commonly mentioned candidates for the prestigious award of being the greatest innovation of all kind include fire, the wheel, the nail, optical lenses, the compass, paper, gunpowder, the printing press, electricity, the steam engine, the internal combustion engine, the telephone, the light bulb, penicillin, vaccination, airplanes, contraceptives, rockets, nuclear fission, semiconductors, the Internet, and many others. The list is endless, and the answer you get will depend on who you ask.

An article in National Geographic[1] points out the ten most important innovations by referring to a list provided by the US librarian of Congress. According to this article, the ten most important innovations in the history of humanity are the printing

---

[1]http://www.nationalgeographic.com/magazine/2017/06/explore-top-ten-innovations/

press, the light bulb, the airplane, the personal computer, vaccines, the automobile, the clock, the telephone, refrigeration, and the camera. The list duly mentions that the task is difficult and that there are no easy and unquestionable answers to this question.

It is remarkable that when searching for conclusions about the most important innovations in the history of humanity, there is a distinct bias toward technological innovations. This bias is perhaps a natural effect from the fact that the world still is in its industrial society era where manufacturing of physical goods is the most important objective for societies and companies. The industrial era from late 1800s all through the 1900s seems to have made us strongly favor and acknowledge hard technologies over social innovations.

It is without doubt that technological innovations have changed the history of humanity to a large extent, but it would be outright incorrect if we did not see the importance of social innovations when trying to understand how innovations have changed the history of humanity. I would even argue that social innovations have played a greater role in this respect than technological innovations.

One example of a list of innovations that also looks at social innovations—i.e., ideas that change how we live and how we understand life—is that provided by the Startup Guide.[2] This list includes not only the examples mentioned above but also social ideas such as language, trade and specialization, farming, legal systems, the alphabet, and (here it comes) money. It would be unfair and incorrect if we did not add ideologies like socialism and capitalism to this list. Just think of how political ideologies like socialism and capitalism—for good and bad—changed the world during the twentieth century. The way we understand the global world is tightly connected to an ideological—and unfortunately often also political and military—fight between social ideas of how we should structure our societies. Leaving the judgment of which ideology that is superior to you, I simply conclude that innovation of ideas has had and have a strong influence on our societies. And I have not even mentioned religion! Well, this is not a book about religion or political ideologies so I will stop here and turn to the topic of this book—the social innovation called money.

So, my argument is that one of the most important social innovations in the history of humanity is money. But what is money? A common definition of money is: "A current medium of exchange in the form of coins and banknotes; coins and banknotes collectively."[3] If you ask a central bank, they could define it as: "Money in the modern economy is just a special form of IOU, or in the language of economic accounts, a financial asset."[4] The simple definition of central bank money is then that it is a document acknowledging that the central bank owes the holder the amount that is specified on the bill or coin. A bill is an IOU from the central bank to the holder. It

---

[2]http://startupguide.com/world/the-40-greatest-innovations-of-all-time/

[3]https://en.oxforddictionaries.com/definition/money

[4]http://www.bankofengland.co.uk/publications/Documents/quarterlybulletin/2014/
qb14q1prereleasemoneyintro.pdf

should be acknowledged that this is a strong simplification—probably too simplified if you ask an economist.[5] But this is what money is—a promise that the bills or coins can be exchanged with something—a cup of coffee or a trip to Chiang Mai in Thailand, issued by a central bank which is backed by a government.

But, as stated previously: "Money is first and foremost a social convention, which emerges to build trust among strangers in their economic transactions, both intertemporal and in spot markets. A convention of monetary exchange facilitates valuable intertemporal exchanges that would not occur otherwise."[6] Money is a tool that help people make transactions in a trustful way. If I hand over my bike to a stranger and he gives me five 100 euro notes in exchange, I can relax. And be happy because that old bike was not worth 500 euros if you ask me. Money enables us to make transactions in a safe way even with people or companies we do not really trust. This is great. In fact, it is a strike of geniality.

And money is one main explanation to how our societies work today. The inventions of writing and grammar made it possible to communicate across distances and over time. Money made it possible to store value and allow exchanges to be independent of time. In a true barter economy, transactions need to be done by exchanging goods and services in real time with the exception that mutual trust could allow exchanges to become independent of time. I can give you 100 kilo of wheat if I can trust you give me 50 kilo of corn 2 months from now. But money is even better since it completes the transaction immediately instead of in 2 months. Money is a prerequisite for trade which stimulates specialization and further trade and so on. Our modern economy is built on trustworthy money and has money as one of its fundamental foundations.

Money is fundamentally an idea that if you provide something—a good or a service—to someone today, you want to trust that someone will provide something for you tomorrow. Nobody—or at least very few—wants to be the person who always gives and gives but never gets something in return. At least not in the long run. We want to trust that giving something away today will mean that we get something back tomorrow. This is a simple but very basic need for everyone. And money is the solution to this problem. If you get money for that which you provide today, you can use this money and buy what you need tomorrow. It is as simple—but at the same time extremely difficult—as that.

The economists would say that effective money must meet three functions. First, money should function as a means of payments—it should enable people to make economic transactions. Second, it should be a unit of account or standard of value—it should help us compare the value of completely different products and services. This makes it possible to compare the value of a cup of coffee and a haircut and thus simplifies our lives and choices. Third, it should serve as a store of value—we should be certain that the value of the money we have is stable. We do

---

[5]For a discussion of what money is, see, for example, Krugman, Paul (2010), "What Is Money?," *New York Times*, December 15th edition.

[6]http //www.riksbank.se/Documents/Rapporter/POV/2017/rap_pov_artikel_6_170120_eng.pdf

not want our well-earned savings of 1000 dollars to buy us a great computer today but only a half-bad computer in a month. And, in the long run, it is not good if the opposite occur either since this will tend to stifle our economies. So, stability of the value of money is critical for it to be effective as a way of making payments. Note that I am talking about money as a tool for economic exchange, i.e., for making payments. There is a much more complex story of the role stability of money has for our economies as a whole, but that is not the topic of this book.

If you are speculating in the value of money—USD or euro—you of course want fluctuation of its value, but that is a different story too. Fluctuation of value makes it possible to gain—just follow the old trick about buy low and sell high—which is critical for investors. Note that doing it the other way around—buy high and sell low—is not recommended even if we daily see that even very professional investors do this. But enough about speculation, let us turn back to money as a tool for exchange.

The functionality of money, i.e., trust in a future return, is arguably (at least if you ask me) one of the most important innovations in the history of humanity and what has enabled us to create advanced societies built on, for instance, technological innovations. Without money there would most likely be very few, if any, techno-logical innovations. Without solid proof, this book is built on the firm belief that money is one of the most important innovations in the history of humanity and therefore worth exploring further, especially as the shape of money is currently being transformed into something very different from what we are used to.

Note that money will *not* disappear if cash disappears! This is often the belief and an indication of the strong influence cash has had on our societies. Many tend to believe that cash is money, but cash is just one form of money even if it has (or had if we talk about Sweden) a critical role in our societies. People tend to think of money only in the form of cash which is partly correct but in the end ultimately incorrect. This book shows that money will remain but cash may disappear. You can think of cash as one of several instruments to provide money and to enable payments. Others include, for instance, card payments, mobile payments, checks, coupons, and Inter-net banking transactions.

There are in fact several fundamentally different forms of money today. The most important form is money backed by a central bank which come in the form of bills or coins. This is a debt the central bank has to the holder of a bill or a coin. This is also what we tend to associate with money even if this form is challenged and thus is losing its predominance in the field of money. The value of this form of money is in Sweden around 1% of GDP and can therefore no longer be seen as an important form of money. It still plays an important role, of course, but not the central role it used to have. Another and more important form of money is bank money, i.e., money that rests in bank accounts and represents a debt from the bank to you. This form of money—what is called bank money—is much more important than cash in our modern societies.

Bank money is actually created by banks as they use collateral that is monetized by being a security for loans that banks provide to companies and people. A bank can create new money by lending to a person with this person's house, apartment or business as security. If the person lends 100,000 euros and uses her house as security, the economy has been boosted with 100,000 new euros. This story can continue as long as the bank makes good judgment of the value of the collateral and does not hand out loans with poor security. But as history has proven over and over again, this ultimately tends to lead to crashes where the newly created money disappears, banks make credit losses, and people and/or businesses end up in financial distress. Bank money is fluctuating depending on the belief in the general economy and the bank's ability to make correct decisions on the future value of the securities they use to provide loans.

A third form of money is virtual currencies which rests on fundamentally different systems and processes constituting trust and value. Yet others include central bank digital currencies (CBDC) and local currencies not backed by a central bank. But we will leave those aside for the time being and come back to them later in a discussion of paradigms of money.

We conclude that cash is being challenged as a central tool for making payments and that our traditionally cash-based societies are being transformed into—more or less—cashless societies. This is what the book aims to understand by looking at how Sweden—the most cashless society in the world—has been transformed during the last decades. The book will not merely do that but also take a look into the future and discuss what we may expect in the coming years.

I acknowledge that the use of cash still is high—and perhaps even increasing—in many parts of the world which shows that development always has to be understood in its context. There may be economic factors influencing the development which has been seen in Spain where cash withdrawals decreased substantially after the financial crisis in 2008 but started to grow again in 2013.[7] But also governmental plans to reduce cash which we saw in India in 2016[8] where around 86% of the cash-in-circulation was declared invalid almost overnight as an attempt to reduce tax evasion and the use of black money in the economy. The attempt did not prove successful, however, as Indians seem to prefer cash and did not change habits overnight.[9] We also tend to see that the use of cash differs between rather similar countries like Sweden and Germany where cash still is very popular in Germany while at the same time disappearing in Sweden and between urban and rural areas where the use of cash tends to be higher in rural areas than in larger cities. In essence, the development in Sweden must be understood through understanding the context of Sweden.

---

[7]https://sdw.ecb.europa.eu/reports.do?node=100000760

[8]https://www.bbc.com/news/world-asia-india-37974423

[9]https://qz.com/india/1127614/demonetisation-indias-grand-plan-to-go-cashless-has-failed/

And to understand the presence and the future, we must also understand the past. This is what I will turn to now.

Chapter 2
History of Money: In the Eye of the Beholder

Why should a book about the future start in a journey into the past? Well simply we cannot understand possible futures if we do not understand the past. One of the first things you learn when doing scenario analysis—studies of potential futures—is that the secret to the future rests in the past. The future will not be like the past since it almost by definition will be different from the past, but the future will be shaped by the past.

A digital society will be based on the institutions that were created for the industrial society even if these institutions over time will be adapted to and perhaps replaced as the digital society will be in need of new forms of institutions affecting societies and people all over the world.

A cashless society will be created on top of the society that was formed for a cash-based economy. The speed of the transition toward less cash and the creation of institutions for a cashless society are built on old systems. The way we perceive money, central banks, payments for transactions, savings, success, and wealth (among other things) will be gradually changed—but not radically—as cash disappears and other forms of money takes its place.

This is exactly why cryptocurrencies meet challenges in becoming payment services for the common man and woman. I am not saying that these currencies never will overcome such challenges but I do acknowledge they exist. The idea of bitcoin—another interesting social invention or perhaps innovation—promoted by Satoshi Nakamoto and others where we get rid of middlemen such as central banks and commercial banks is radical, provocative, and therefore highly interesting. But this is not enough to make it an automatic success. The current monetary system has a lot of institutions that become problems or even barriers to the introduction of bitcoin and other cryptocurrencies. Thus in order to understand the transformation of money, we must first turn to the history of money.

© The Author(s) 2019
N. Arvidsson, *Building a Cashless Society*, SpringerBriefs in Economics,
https://doi.org/10.1007/978-3-030-10689-8_2

The Birth of Historic Forms of Money

It is difficult to pinpoint when the first versions of money were put in use and historians provide different accounts. We know there has been sophisticated systems guiding trade for many thousand years even long before money in the form of coins were created. It is such systems governing exchange and value that led to what we today call money.[1] I must acknowledge that when researching money, I am regularly contacted by researchers and people that have various claims on when money first was used which indicates there are many different views on the history of money.

One early use of money has been connected to the economic system of Mesopotamia around 3500 years ago. Historians have found coins issued by the king Ammi-Ditana, who ruled Mesopotamia in the period 1683–1647 BC, that were made of clay. The coins had inscriptions saying they could be exchanged with a certain amount of corn and that this exchange was guaranteed by the king (Ferguson, 2008). This foundation of money is the same with what we have today where central banks—and in the end the government of a nation—guarantee the value of money. There have of course also been other ways to guarantee the value of money such as metal-based coins. One early version of bills has been connected to the Tang dynasty in China where deposits of coins or metals with the state were proven via a paper-based receipt that in essence became a promissory note issued by the state and that therefore could be used as a means of payments between other parties. The low weight and possibility to make high-value payments in an efficient way made such notes attractive by merchants, and increasingly popular in societies at large.

Money in various shapes and forms has evidently been used for 5000 years and started in Mesopotamia and Egypt and then spread over the world as an important prerequisite for trade and economic development. In 250 BC, coinage in gold, silver, and bronze had become a dominant form of money in large parts of the Mediterranean, the Near East, and India (Williams, 1997). The spread of money in the Mediterranean area was strengthened by the Roman Empire as it became aware of the importance of money for growth and expansion when they realized the limits of barter trade. This is evident in the claim that the Latin word for money, *pecunia*, is derived from the Latin word for cattle, *pecus*, since cattle often was used in barter trade in the early days of the Roman Empire (Williams, 1997, p. 39). This is yet another indication and illustration of the importance money has had for efficient trade and economic development.

Throughout the history of humanity, we have seen many different monetary systems that have been strong and later failed because of the underlying challenge of the provider—a king or a state—to guarantee the value of the money they have issued. Examples include Rome's coins during the Roman Empire, Spanish gold coins during the 1500s and 1600s, German inflation in the 1920s after the WW1.

---

[1]See, for instance, https://www.britishmuseum.org/explore/themes/money/the_beginnings_of_money.aspx

Brazilian money in the 1980s and 1990s, and the hyperinflation in Zimbabwe in 2008. The case of Zimbabwe is especially interesting as the monthly inflation reached an unprecedented and incomprehensible 79.6 billion percent in November 2008 which was halted when people—for obvious reasons—stopped using this currency (Hanke & Kwok, 2009)! Another but less spectacular case is Sweden that had high inflation in the 1970s based on the government's inability to stabilize the economy. The list of examples is endless. It is evidently not easy to maintain monetary stability and trustworthy payment systems over longer periods of time.

Today we take state-backed bills and coins for granted where the value of such money is based on the economic performance of the state and the credibility behind the promise that money has a certain value. Cash has a long and strong history where Sweden was one of the first countries to launch government-supported cash in its current form and now potentially may become one of the first to stop issuing government-supported cash.

To understand what is really happening, we must provide a deeper analysis than just look at cash and the ongoing transformation into cashless societies. I will therefore turn to a discussion of three paradigms—or fundamental principles—of money.

Three Paradigms of Money

An insightful way to understand the history of money is to analyze the fundamental principles behind each manifestation of money. An often used—and often misused—concept when performing such an analysis is a paradigm[2] approach. In his famous book about scientific paradigms, Kuhn (2012) defines a scientific paradigm in a broad sense as "the entire constellation of beliefs, values and techniques shared by members of a scientific community" and in a more narrow sense as "universally recognized scientific achievements that provide model problems and solutions to a community of practitioners" (ibid).

The essence of a paradigm is that there are some fundamental principles, values, and approaches to problems and solutions that differ between different paradigms. Kuhn discusses scientific paradigms with a specific focus on natural science and provides examples such as the difference between a paradigm resting on the assumption that earth is the center of the universe and all other planets circle around earth and a paradigm assuming the sun is the center of one solar system and that all planets in this system—such as earth—circle around the sun. Depending on which starting point you have, you will understand space and planets differently. Another feature of paradigms is that they tend to be mutually exclusive. You cannot believe

---

[2]The word paradigm comes from Greek and means "a typical example or pattern of something; a pattern or model" according to the Oxford English Dictionary https://en.oxforddictionaries.com/

Fig. 2.1 Paradigm. Source:
author's own illustration

that the sun circles around the earth and that the earth circles around the sun at the same time.

And the examples of such paradigmatic differences are abound. Do you believe that God created life on Earth as we know it today or that evolution did? These are different paradigms—or cognitive models—for how to understand the creation of life on Earth. In the strict sense, paradigms are mutually exclusive and not possible to integrate and combine. In a Kuhnian sense, you cannot believe in both creationism and in evolution at the same time. You must choose. Why? Because the fundamental principles and assumptions are incoherent and contradictive. From a strict paradigmatic standpoint, it is not possible to believe both that God created life and that life somehow was created through evolution. Some tend to believe in one paradigm and others in another. And the idea of paradigms can be applied to technologies and money as well (Fig. 2.1).

Kuhn argued that science should prove what it assumes while Popper argued the opposite, i.e., that science should test and disprove that which is taken for granted. Lakatos' integrated Kuhn and Popper by suggesting there are research programs in which some core ideas should not easily be challenged while more peripheral ideas should be challenged (Chalmers, 2013). This illustrates the challenge we face when aiming to understand ideas. Now, this is not a book in philosophy of science and we can leave this discussion aside. Let me just take the concept of paradigms into a discussion of technological dimensions of different representations of money. This will follow an approach introduced by Dosi (1982) who suggested that technological systems can be understood in a similar way as we understand scientific paradigms.

Dosi argues that "the procedures and the nature of 'technologies' are suggested to broadly similar to those which characterize 'science'. In particular, there appear to 'technological paradigms' (or research programmes) performing a similar role to 'scientific paradigms' (or research programmes)" (Dosi, 1982).

This implies that we can understand a particular technology or technological field as a paradigm being built on a combination of fundamental principles and values that makes it different from other competing paradigms. We see such battles between technological paradigms regularly in different industries such as those related to nonrenewable versus renewable energy, those related to internal combustion engines versus electric engines, those related to writing on typewriters, versus those related to writing on a personal computer, and so on. Each of these being characterized by particular features related to technological system, need of input factors, logistical systems, production processes, prices, principles of use, but also underlying values related to whether the technology is regarded to efficient, reliable, environmentally friendly, and cool and in other ways deemed better than the alternative. The paradigm is thus not only about technology but also involve organizational principles and subjective emotions connected to it.

Depending on which paradigm you—consciously or unconsciously—belong to, you will see different things when studying a phenomenon. A socialist will see injustice when a person is richer than another person, while the capitalist will see this as a fair distribution of wealth based on each person's abilities and efforts. And given the ideological paradigms each person believes in, each person is entirely correct in relation to the paradigm. In addition they will have problems discussing this. The socialist will use socialist ideology to convince the capitalist, and the capitalist will use capitalist ideology to convince the socialist. Will they be able to come to shared solution? No, probably not. At least not as long as they do not acknowledge some of the basic ideas and concepts in the other person's ideology. But they can of course still live side by side and survive in the same democratic society.

The viewpoint shaped by paradigms can be illustrated by the classical Penrose stairs.[3] Where does it start? Which part is on top of the other? What do you see? Once you have decided, it may be difficult to change the viewpoint.

It is the same with money. We can see different paradigms of money that live side by side in the same economy. There are different technological paradigms connected to money. To be more precise, I will argue there are three different technological paradigms connected to money: value-based money, fiat[4] money, and decentralized money. And they live side by side with each other even if fiat money is dominating the scene. So what do I mean with this?

Value-Based Money

Value-based money is money whose value is based on the inherent value of the metal on which it is based. This includes gold coins, silver coins, bronze coins, and well in fact any type of coin where the value is based on the value of the material it is made of. Value-based money was dominating the monetary scene for thousands of years starting in the third millennium BC (Williams, 1997). This technological paradigm is very intuitive since anyone who receives a coin that has a certain weight and is made of a certain grade of a certain metal can estimate the value of the coin by knowing the price of that metal. The holder of a coin can melt it and sell it as metal for a certain price per kilo (or whatever measure of weight that is used). This technological paradigm is simple and straightforward, and therefore often used, but it is of course not without challenges and problems.

---

[3]https://en.wikipedia.org/wiki/Penrose_stairs

[4]Fiat comes from Latin and means "let it be done." When it comes to money, this means that the value of a certain type of money – a currency – cannot be decided by the provider of this money like a central bank. The value will live its (close to) own life and will be decided by the users in a market. The value will "be done" by the users. https://en.oxforddictionaries.com/definition/fiat

Fig. 2.2 Gold—a source to value-based money. Source: https://www.riksbank.se/imagevault/publishedmedia/6343vlh0uge9jpqihaxf/Guldtackor.jpg

There are countless ways to trick the system and thereby make unjustified gains. One can manipulate the metal content, the size and weight of the coin, and the symbols imprinted on the coin. Why not have a thin layer of a precious metal on the surface and then a center made of a cheap metal? Then hoping the receiver will not check this. In short, any way to trick the receiver into believing the coin is worth more than it actually is—without being caught—can lead to gains beyond that which is motivated by the transaction in itself. Another problem is the practical use, which can be exemplified by the almost 20-kilo heavy bronze coin that was produced in Sweden in 1644–1645.[5] Not very convenient for anyone. Folklore also tell us about the quadratic coins with sharp corners that allegedly created holes in pockets, fell out, and was lost, yet another kind of practical problem with value-based coins and perhaps the reason why they are round today (Fig. 2.2).

Fiat Money

Our second technological paradigm connect to money is fiat money. Here the value of money is based on the trust we put in the producer of money and his or her ability to deliver the promise that lies in the value of the money printed on it. As many

---

[5]http://www.myntkabinettet.se/fakta/foremalsfakta/platmynt

innovations, fiat money grew from the realization that it had advantages that its proceeding competitor—value-based money—did not have. Value-based coins were somewhat inconvenient to carry around and to safeguard which meant that it could be advantageous to develop other forms of money. Paper money as we know it today is claimed to have been invented in China in 1189 AD (Williams, 1997, p. 149) when the ruler realized paper is an interesting way to produce money. Paper is much easier to carry around and to produce even if it—on the other hand—also is easier to destroy. A simple match will do a good job.

At first, paper money was basically a receipt for the underlying value of a security—like the gold that was deposited in a vault—but it soon changed character. Realizing the ease with which money now could be transferred between business-men if compared to weighty coins, people soon started to set a premium value on paper money. All of a sudden a 100 daler bill became more worth than 100 daler in copper coins. The ease with which money could be stored and used meant a premium in addition to the metal value of the security the paper originally was built on. Seignorage was born.[6]

That is quite remarkable! How could a paper saying it is worth 100 daler be worth more than copper worth 100 daler? And how could a paper saying it is worth 100 daler all of a sudden be worth more than 100 daler? It all boils down to the ease with which it is used and the trust users put in the provider of these papers.

This also became the foundation of a radical transformation of money. Paper not only made trade easier but it also laid the foundation for money as we know it today, i.e., cash. Here it is the trust in the writing and in the signatures on the paper that is the foundation for how much we think the paper—the bill—is worth. If it says 500 euro and this is guaranteed by the European Central Bank, we believe this and are ready to hand over our bike to a stranger if we get this piece of paper in return. Amazing. If it says 20 SEK, we can get a (half-decent) cup of coffee in Sweden if we hand it over to a café owner. To also get a (half-decent) cinnamon roll, you will need one more bill saying 20 SEK. This is the essence of fiat money—we trust the numbers written on a piece of paper if it is guaranteed by a central bank and backed by a government.

The trust does not come from heaven though and we have seen many examples of what happens when trust is lost. High inflation is a typical indicator of when people have lost their trust in the central bank to uphold the value of the bills they have produced. It takes hard and stubborn work from a government and its central bank to keep the trust and remain a low-inflation country and currency. This is important to remember as we today live in a low-inflation era! (Fig. 2.3)

---

[6]Seignorage is based on revenues that a central bank receives on its coins and banknotes. Equivalent to the return on a central bank's assets corresponding to banknotes and coins in circulation less the central bank's total costs for cash management. http://www.riksbank.se/en/Glossary/#S

Fig. 2.3 Examples of fiat money. Source: author's own illustration

Decentralized Money

The third paradigm is what I will call decentralized money. You would probably call it bitcoin, Ethereum, cryptocurrencies, or virtual currencies. Or digital money. Or you are perhaps calling it the future of money free from central banks, banks, and other inconvenient and expensive middlemen? No matter which name you prefer, the essence of this paradigm lies in the decentralization of control and authentification. Let's say we had cash whose authenticity and validity was guaranteed by the community of users instead of by a central bank. That is the principle that bitcoin is based on (but in a digital form).

Bitcoin actually has physical coins too, but the essence of bitcoin is digitalized tokens whose authenticity is controlled by a decentralized ledger accessible by every user of the coin. This ledger keeps stock of transactions and thereby control that bitcoin are genuine and not fake. It is this decentralized ledger that is the essence of the money in the system. And the ledger, which is built on the technology called block chain, is transparent for every user of the system (or at least transparent for their computers). This turns control into a shared responsibility by all users and thus also means that middlemen—central banks and commercial banks—no longer are needed. This in turn means that middlemen fees can be avoided.

It is interesting to note that the bitcoin story starts from the idea of money as value-based money, i.e., the first paradigm outlined above. When Satoshi Nakamoto wrote the conceptual paper that structures the foundation of bitcoin, he or she based it on the analogy of gold. Yes. Gold. The rare metal. The virtual currency bitcoin is built on the idea of a metal found in the ground. This is interesting. Perhaps Satoshi Nakamoto is like King Midas who could create gold from out of plain air by just touching it with the exception that Nakamoto found a way to get around the problem that even the food King Midas was to eat turned into gold before he could swallow it. Satoshi Nakamoto avoided this by making it digital. Smart.

This is how Satoshi Nakamoto summarized the article:

A purely peer-to-peer version of electronic cash would allow online payments to be sent directly from one party to another without going through a financial institution. Digital signatures provide part of the solution, but the main benefits are lost if a trusted third party is still required to prevent double-spending. We propose a solution to the double-spending problem using a peer-to-peer network. The network timestamps transactions by hashing them into an ongoing chain of hash-based proof-of-work, forming a record that cannot be changed without redoing the proof-of-work. The longest chain not only serves as proof of the sequence of events witnessed, but proof that it came from the largest pool of CPU power. As long as a majority of CPU power is controlled by nodes that are not cooperating to attack the network, they'll generate the longest chain and outpace attackers. The network itself requires minimal structure. Messages are broadcast on a best effort basis, and nodes can leave and rejoin the network at will, accepting the longest proof-of-work chain as proof of what happened while they were gone (Nakamoto, 2008, p. 1).

There are several important things that are worth mentioning when trying to understand what bitcoin is. One critical is that which is called a peer-to-peer system. Nakamoto believes that one of the most critical problems with the current structure of money—the fiat money paradigm—is that it needs middlemen, financial institutions, to control transactions and authenticity of money.

The aim of bitcoin is to build a system where all actors in the system can control it since the digital information contains data about the value of the payment and the authenticity of money, which can be controlled by the receiver—or rather the receiver's computer—when receiving the payment. Since all information about all payments exist in the network of computers that are using bitcoin, the control and information is accessible to all. No need to trust—and pay!—a middleman. This system is called a decentralized ledger that contains information about previous transactions, and this record is used to check history and authenticity of each payment.

In the old days, hotels ran ledgers where all information about guests were written and stored. This information was then accessible to all that had access to the ledger. The digital version is built on the same idea except that the ledgers behind bitcoin are accessible by all.

What then is a block chain? The simple version is that one payment using bitcoin creates a block with information about value, the payer, and the payee, and a collection of blocks create a block chain. The block chain is available to all users in the system and can thereby be controlled by all nodes in the system. Decentralization of information about transactions and holders guarantees transparency and is the foundation for security and protection against double-spend, hacking, and forged transactions—at least in theory.

If, however, someone can control the system, there is a hypothetic opportunity to change the decentralized information in the block chain. No matter whether the security in a decentralized ledger is higher or lower than in a traditional electronic system with middlemen and regulation, it is without doubt that this new technological and new institutional logic offers an interesting and promising alternative to our current systems. But—as in any system built on digital platforms—it is critical to attract users to build interoperability and efficiency.

Luckily enough, Satoshi Nakamoto also knew one or two things about marketing! Even today there is no official information regarding who the person Satoshi Nakamoto is. Rumors fly around and several persons have been pointed out to be

Satoshi Nakamoto,[7] but at the end of the day, we do not know. We do know that he or she is rich, however. He or she is thought to own about 1 million bitcoin or more. But leaving that aside, I was talking about marketing. If you want to create a hype, why not have a creator that remains a mystery person and then putting him—because the mythical Satoshi Nakamoto is a man—on a pedestal and follow his seminal paper (to all you researchers: this is really a seminal paper!) as if it is written in stone. Smart. Ingenious.

And really strange given that the ruling principle of the dominating paradigm of money—fiat money—is that we know exactly who is providing the money. In this new paradigm, it is an anonymous system that generates new money via a predetermined but self-regulatory process.

Bitcoin is thought of as gold, i.e., something that already exists but needs to be mined in order to be usable and valuable. So I guess Satoshi Nakamoto is not entirely like King Midas since he could create new gold. There is an upper limit of how much bitcoin that can exist which is set at 21 million bitcoin. In theory there will never be more than 21 million bitcoin.

When I write this text,[8] the total number of bitcoins are 17.4 million and each bitcoin is worth 5507 US dollars, which means that the value of all bitcoin in circulation is around 96 billion US dollars or around 85 billion euro. This is comparable to the value of all US dollar in circulation which was 1463 billion US dollars in the end of 2016[9] and all euro in circulation which was 1147 billion euro in January 2018.[10] Acknowledging the problem that there are some time lags in these comparisons, the total value of bitcoins in circulation is currently well below 10% of the total value of euros in circulation. These numbers will of course not be entirely correct when you read this book so I recommend you to check the numbers at: www. coindesk.com or www.bitcoin.com (Fig. 2.4).

The analogy of gold does not end there, however. In order to control authenticity and transactions, you need a lot of computing power and this is also supplied via a network of distributed computers, i.e., the computers connected to the network. To incentivize this access, a person who allows the system to use his or her computer (s) will be rewarded by new bitcoins. This is called mining—the gold analogy continues—and the persons are called miners. Mining in the digital world is radically different from that in the old world though. The traditional gold miners got wet, had guns, and ate beans, while the modern ones get tired, have computers, and drink energy drinks. Even a traditionally physical task like digging out the earth to extract metal has been given its digital version in the cryptocurrency community. And there are even physical coins representing the cryptocurrency bitcoin. It is evident that the physical reality also has an important role to play in a digital world.

---

[7]See: https://www.coindesk.com/information/who-is-satoshi-nakamoto/

[8]November 15 2018 via www.bitcoin.com

[9]https://www.federalreserve.gov/paymentsystems/coin_currcircvalue.htm

[10]https://www.ecb.europa.eu/stats/policy_and_exchange_rates/banknotes+coins/circulation/html/index.en.html

Fig. 2.4 Approximate bitcoin price fluctuations versus US dollars. Source: https://markets.bitcoin.com/crypto/BTC (numbers based on prices quoted on www.markets.bitcoin.com/crypto/btc)

The limit of the total number of bitcoin that can exist aims at making it impossible to create inflation in the system. It will not be possible to create new bitcoins once the 21 million ceiling is met, which is projected to happen sometime around 2140,[11] i.e., around 122 years from now. This will make it impossible to create new money, contrary to what we see central banks and commercial banks do all the time when they need to and are able to.

The aim is to set a predefined limit of how many bitcoin can exist. It is not clear, however, into how many decimals a bitcoin can be divided, which in practice makes the 21 million ceiling unclear. As of today the smallest amount is one hundred millionth of a bitcoin which is called one satoshi. So one satoshi is 0.0001 bitcoin. Yes, it is named after the founder Satoshi Nakamoto. In practice this means the number of satoshis can be up to 210 billion coins.

As we saw above, the total value of all bitcoins is less than 10% of all euros in circulation. Not bad for a currency that is 10 years old.

Why do I call it a currency? Well, because it is. I would argue that bitcoin has not yet become a competitive payment services—it is a virtual currency that may become a competitive and well-used payment service. To explain what I mean, I will turn back to my discussion of paradigms of money or different systems and logics behind money.

---

[11] https://cryptocoinmastery.com/what-happens-when-all-bitcoins-have-been-mined/

Understanding the Three Paradigms of Money

There are three different paradigms of money: value-based, fiat, and decentralized. Based on the three fundamental functions of money, means of payment, unit of account, and store of value, I have outlined the three paradigms of money in Table 2.1.

I conclude this analysis of paradigms of money by stating that we cannot understand and compare value-based money, fiat money, and decentralized money if we do not understand the paradigmatic differences between them. If a virtual currency like bitcoin—in its current version—is to replace fiat money like SEK, we need to see a drastic paradigm shift in the way we perceive money, and this shift would require most financial markets as well as commodity markets to transform the way they set prices, calculate risks, and perform transactions. This can of course happen, but it is likely to require some time until the majority of business actors have done it. Another—and probably more important—part of such a paradigm shift is that the fundamental financial and monetary policies must change.

An important tool to handle the economy for any government relates to money. By setting interest rates on sovereign bonds, the government and a central bank can influence the development of the economy. If bitcoin based on decentralized ledgers constituted the money used for all or most transactions, the government would have lost central parts of its power to control the local economy. They could still try to influence the value of bitcoin via open market operations, but this would then be directed to a global currency and not a domestic one. The effects from currency fluctuations of a global currency like bitcoin will of course have unclear effects on a local market such as Sweden or the European Union. Thus, this potential shift is not only about money, but it is also about the power of governments.

To be effective, bitcoin would also have to meet a comparable level in each of the three character dimensions in Table 2.1. Overall these factors explain why there is so much interest and emotions—from enthusiasm to fear—related to cryptocurrencies based on decentralized ledgers.

But it is very clear that even though decentralized money is still in its infancy, this phenomenon is challenging the way we understand money. To cite Camera (2017)[12]: "The institution of money is rapidly evolving thanks to the development in computer-based cryptography." We may not yet know exactly how this new form of money—decentralized money—will play out, but we can be certain it will change the history of money!

---

[12]https://www.riksbank.se/globalassets/media/rapporter/pov/artiklar/svenska/2017/170120/rap_pov_artikel_6_170120_sve.pdf

Table 2.1 Three paradigms of money

	Value-based money[a]	Fiat money	Decentralized money
Critical assumptions and underlying beliefs: means of payment	Is based on the liquidity in markets for the metal upon which the money is based and the ease with which the coin can be melted and sold as metal. Even bills have been directly connected to a certain amount of metal (gold) and thereby regarded as value-based money[b]	Is based on the trust users have in the provider, i.e., a central bank backed by the government and the authenticity of the money. The provider backs the money and guarantees its usability. This is institutionalized in central bank law stating that cash is legal tender. Strong institutions safeguarding fiat money makes it possible to use in almost in all situations. The value of fiat money is connected to the trust users have in the state's monetary policies.	This is based on the trust users have in the decentralized ledger that is underlying the money and the liquidity of the virtual currency on the money markets. It is assumed that the technological system is guaranteeing the money
Critical assumptions and underlying beliefs: unit of account	This is determined by the number of users that set prices in the currency and relate their idea of the value of a good or service in the metal underlying coins and bills	This is a de facto standard as a unit of account in the geographic area in which the currency is legal tender. Taxes, fees for public services, fines, and other publically available services are priced in the currency. In the end, it is determined by the number of users that set prices in the fiat currency	This is determined by the number of users that set their prices of a good or service in the virtual currency
Critical assumptions and underlying beliefs: store of value	Is based on the fluctuation of metal values. This implies that the store of value of the money is directly connected to the supply and demand of the metal that the money is based on	First the trust that the central bank and the government create around the economic situation of the country in general and its money. Second, the economic policies governing the currency	Is based on the currency fluctuation of the virtual currency, which in turn is based on supply and demand of the virtual currency

(continued)

Table 2.1 (continued)

	Value-based money[a]	Fiat money	Decentralized money
		exchange rate. Third, regulation and licenses around the companies providing services and consumer protection for deposits with these companies	

[a]In this example I discuss value-based money as if it was based on the value of gold, i.e., the traditional circumstance that one could melt the coin and sell it as gold. This is of course not entirely correct today but still used to exemplify the differences between the three paradigms

[b]Paper money that is classified as value-based can be exemplified by the early deposit notes in Sweden in the seventeenth century or when currencies were directly tied to the value of gold in the Bretton-Woods era in the twentieth century

References

Camera, G. (2017). *A perspective on electronic alternatives to traditional currencies* (Penning och valutapolitik 2017:1). Stockholm: The Riksbank.

Chalmers, A. F. (2013). *What is this thing called science?* Indianapolis, IN: Hackett Publishing.

Dosi, G. (1982). Technological paradigms and technological trajectories—A suggested interpretation of the determinants and directions of technical change. *Research Policy, 11*, 147–162.

Ferguson, N. (2008). *The ascent of money: A financial history of the world*. London: Penguin.

Hanke, S. H., & Kwok, A. K. F. (2009). On the measurement of Zimbabwe's hyperinflation. *Cato Journal, 29*, No. 2 (Spring/Summer 2009).

Kuhn, T. S. (2012). *The structure of scientific revolutions*. Chicago, IL: University of Chicago Press.

Nakamoto, S. (2008). *Bitcoin: A peer-to-peer electronic cash system*.

Williams, J. (1997). *Money—A history* (J. Williams with J. Cribb & E. Errington, Eds.). London: Published for the Trustees of the British Museum, British Museum Press.

Chapter 3
Cash Payments: An International Comparison

A global trend in retail payments is that noncash transactions grow steadily but that cash transactions still are important—especially when it comes to low-value payments—and even increasing in some countries. The World Payments Report (2017) shows that cash in circulation in relation to GDP decreases in a small number of countries—Sweden, Denmark, the UK, Canada, and South Africa—while overall trend is that this ratio is stable or increasing. The trend is continuing globally where noncash transaction grew globally with 10.1% in 2016 (World Payments Report, 2018).

These report show that noncash transactions grow steadily where debit and credit cards are the dominating services in this growth, while check usage is decreasing. This implies that electronic services are growing steadily even if cash is still an important payment service in many countries. It is also interesting to note that contactless cards have become a standard for cards in many European countries but more importantly that the highest growth rates for noncash transactions are seen in Asia, Eastern Europe, the Middle East, and Africa (World Payments Report, 2017, p. 6).

If we study the patterns in Europe more closely, we see that Sweden is different from other European countries. The use of cash is significantly lower than in other European countries when studying the share of transactions at point of sales (POS), i.e., of transactions done in stores. The share in Sweden is less than 20% where most other countries show number above 50% (Table 3.1). These numbers confirm results from earlier studies such as the one made by the Riksbank[1] showing that Sweden has an extremely low number of cash in circulation in relation to GDP and a relatively high number when it comes to card payments per person and year.

---

[1]https://www.riksbank.se/sv/press-och-publicerat/publikationer/om-finansiell-stabilitet/den-svenska-finansmarknaden/?_t_id=1B2M2Y8AsgTpgAmY7PhCfg%3d%3d&_t_q=svenska
+finansiella+marknaden&_t_tags=language%3asv%2csiteid%3af3366ed3-598f-4166-aa5a-
45d5751e940b&_t_ip=130.237.51.192&_t_hit.id=Riksbanken_Core_Models_Pages_
ArticlePage/_9dda93fb-bb0c-4416-b259-0de7471c3c43_sv&_t_hit.pos=2

© The Author(s) 2019
N. Arvidsson, *Building a Cashless Society*, SpringerBriefs in Economics,
https://doi.org/10.1007/978-3-030-10689-8_3

Table 3.1 The share of
transactions (point of sales) of
cash (in terms of value) in
Europe 2017[a]

Country	Share of POS transactions cash (%)
Sweden	18
Netherlands	27
France	28
Luxembourg	30
Estonia	31
Belgium	32
Finland	33
Ireland	49
Latvia	54
Germany	55
Lithuania	62
Slovakia	66
Austria	67
Spain	68
Italy	68
Slovenia	68
Cyprus	72
Malta	74
Greece	75

Sources: Arvidsson, Hedman, and Segendorf (2018) and Esselink
and Hernández (2017)
[a]The data on Sweden is based on Arvidsson et al. (2018) who did a
survey with Swedish merchants, and the data on all other countries
in the table is based on Esselink and Hernández (2017) who did a
diary-based study with consumers in different countries in the
Euro zone

This short international comparison shows that the low use of cash in Sweden is
atypical. There are other countries showing similar patterns—like Denmark and the
UK—but even compared to these, Sweden has a stronger and faster decline in the
use of cash. One critical explanation is most likely the legal situation in Sweden. It is
perfectly ok for a merchant to say no to cash in Sweden. The system for cash
handling services in Sweden has also been subjugated to outsourcing and privatization which in essence means that vital activities like printing, transportation,
protection, equipment supply, and other services are provided by private companies
like banks, cash-in-transit service companies, depot holders, cash printing companies, and guard service providers. All of these factors have led to a supply and
demand-driven development of the use of cash in Sweden.

I am not saying this is a perfect market in the conventional sense because traditions
in Sweden in combination with the importance of well-functioning multi-sided
platforms have led to a situation where providers do not charge consumers for
using cash. At least not directly. There are no consumer fees for cash services that
influence consumers' choice of which payment service to use. Instead consumers pay
the fees for cash indirectly via annual card fees and—most likely—other less

transparent fees in the banking system. All in all, the decrease in the use of cash happens because it is legally possible and because merchants and consumers tend to prefer other solutions.

References

Arvidsson, N., Hedman, J., & Segendorf, B. (2018). *När slutar svenska handlare acceptera kontanter?* (Handelsrådet, Forskningsrapport 2018:1).
Esselink, H., & Hernández, L. (2017). *The use of cash by households in the euro area.*
World Payments Report 2017 by CapGemini and BNP Paribas.
World Payments Report 2018 by CapGemini and BNP Paribas.

Chapter 4
The Story of Cash and the Route Toward a Cashless Society: The Case of Sweden

History of Swedish Money: From the Tenth Century to the Nineteenth Century

The Swedish[1] payment system can be said to have started in 995 as the first Swedish coins were minted in Sigtuna as a response to an increased trade between European merchants. This helped and stimulated trade between Swedish and foreign merchants and thereby became important for the economy in the cities that made the cornerstones of these societies. However, the system was not well developed until the beginning of the seventeenth century when the first banks were created as the chancellor of the realm Axel Oxenstierna stressed the need for banks that could create a better connection between savings and lending in Sweden. As most of the times, this also was in the interest of the King of Sweden Karl X Gustav who was fighting wars in Poland and in need of money to finance the war efforts.

The King awarded the first rights to start a Swedish bank which came in the form of Stockholm Banco in 1656, which was owned by Johan Palmstruch and regulated by the monarch. This bank soon launched credit notes to expand their credit system which led to good business opportunities for the bank. Palmstruch had launched attractive credit services to an economy that was in need of funding to engage in both military and industrial operations. Stockholm Banco seemed to have hit a perfect time with its attractive financial services. Business bloomed. But as we have become aware of over time, financial services and credits cannot expand too much without a sound base. And this became painstakingly evident also for Palmstruch.

Stockholm Banco apparently became somewhat carried away with their success and started to print more bills than they could cover by reliable securities. A bubble was created that later exploded. As creditors to the bank became aware of the problem, a bank run led to the closure of the bank in 1664. Stockholm Banco could simply not repay its creditors since it had given credit that was not covered

---

[1]Even though it should be noted that a notion of the state of Sweden did not exist at this time.

© The Author(s) 2019
N. Arvidsson, *Building a Cashless Society*, SpringerBriefs in Economics,
https://doi.org/10.1007/978-3-030-10689-8_4

by reliable securities. They faced a situation we still see now and then when banks oversupply credit in order to gain market share and profits.

It is interesting to note that the society of that time was radically tougher than the society today. While today's bankmen face jail sentences or simply mockery in media but generally can leave with a generous compensation package, Johan Palmstruch was sentenced to a death penalty for mismanagement of the bank! Tough times, indeed. It should be noted though that he was later reprieved of this sentence. Seen in this historical light, it is of course very good that our policies regarding financial crimes have changed in a humane direction, but we perhaps not be too sorry for bankmen that misbehave.

The crash of Stockholm Banco led to the creation of a new and highly critical institution in our financial system: the formation of a Swedish central bank. In 1668 the Swedish parliament decided to use the remains of Stockholm Banco to form Riksens Ständers Bank under the ownership and control of the state. This later changed its name to Sveriges Riksbank and became the first central bank in the world.[2] This did not mean that the money and payment system in Sweden became standardized and homogeneous, though. This was not realized until the formation of the 1897 central banking law through which the Sveriges Riksbank was granted a monopoly on issuing banknotes in Sweden, which came into effect in 1904. Up until 1904 it was perfectly possible for a Swedish bank to issue their own banknotes.

The modern Swedish payment system with a central bank issuing the only form of money that is allowed and also backing its value was thus realized in the early twentieth century. Swedish money has then been meeting many different challenges and using many different solutions as being pegged to gold, to the British pound, to the US dollar, and to baskets of currencies in the Bretton Woods system. The Swedish crown (SEK) eventually became fully convertible and floating in 1992 as the government and the Riksbank found it impossible to defend a fixed exchange rate to other currencies. Not even a 500% interest rate from the Riksbank helped not maintain a strong Swedish crown[3]! The Swedish crown has been freely floating ever since.

---

[2]It should be noted that the Bank of England and the Riksbank are competing regarding which one was the first central bank. The first version of the the Riksbank was founded in 1668 (http://www.riksbank.se/en/The-Riksbank/History/Important-date/1590-1668/) while the Bank of England was founded in 1694 (http://www.bankofengland.co.uk/about/Pages/default.aspx).

[3]https://www.riksbank.se/en-gb/about-the-riksbank/history/1900-1999/interest-rate-500%2D%2Dthe-krona-floats/

The Development of the Swedish Payment System During the Last Secades

This story can of course start just about anywhere and I have decided to start in the middle of the twentieth century. This is a time when the Swedish economy has initiated its growth and success after WW2 and is about to becoming one of the richest economies in the world. Industry is booming, employment is high, wages and salaries are rising, exports are soaring, and women are entering the labor markets. The social democratic party is ruling the country and a strong welfare state has been launched and is gaining ground. All in all, it is probably one of the best periods in Sweden ever. And, there are several important technologies that are changing the Swedish society like television, automobiles, telephones, household appliances, and many others. But one technology is especially important when we talk about payments—computers are used in more and more applications all over the society. And more specifically, banks are among the most advanced sectors when it comes to automatizing and computerizing their operations.

In the 1960s, banks have already taking steps to make their operations more efficient by launching systems that can run automated processes to control and administer tasks in the banking system. The banks had seen the potential of these systems and invested in building automated systems to operate accounts and transactions, but they lack one critical component: customers. At this time, wages and salaries are often paid directly from the employer to the employee in cash which means that banks do not have access to these funds and potential customers. The banks see a potential to set up a structure that can benefit employers and employees while at the same time attracting new customers to the banks. The transaction bank account is marketed and the large-scale electronic banking system takes an important step forward.

Companies now start to pay wages and salaries directly to employees' bank accounts (electronically) instead of via cash. The employers save costs, the banks get new customers, unions agree as long as banks do not charge consumers for cash withdrawals, and employees like it. It was a win-win-win case that completely changed banking and laid the foundation—the transaction bank account—that still is the core of the payment system.

The ensuing decades reinforced this new system even if the use of cash grew in real terms. The value of cash in circulation in 1950 was around 10 % of GDP and decreased steadily in the coming decades, but that was mainly because the growth of GDP was higher than the growth of cash in circulation. The value of cash in circulation increased from less than 10 billion SEK in the beginning of 1960 to around 55 billion SEK in 1990. Cash is still popular in the 1990s even if electronic payments are becoming more and more popular (Figs. 4.1 and 4.2).

Two important things then happen in the late 1980s and 1990s. Card companies and banks intensify their efforts to transform cash payments into electronic card payments by offering card payments and by introducing fees to payments based on checks. The banks saw benefits from running more efficient electronic systems

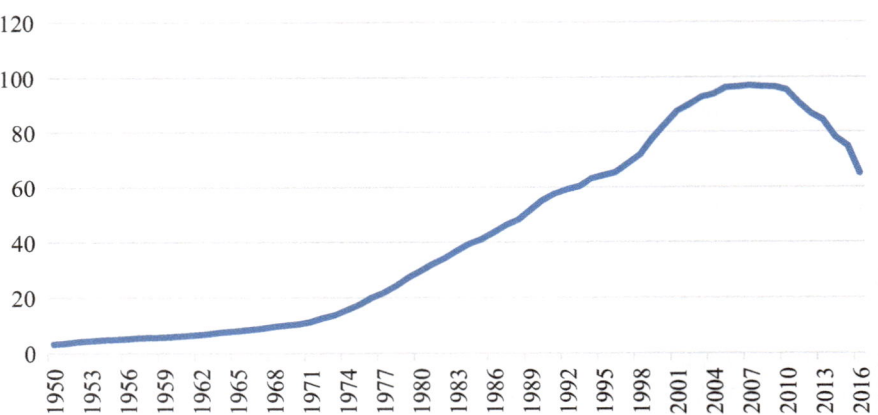

Fig. 4.1 Cash in circulation in Sweden 1950–2016. Source: The Riksbank (https://www.riksbank. se/sv/press-och-publicerat/publikationer/om-finansiell-stabilitet/den-svenska-finansmarknaden/?_ t_id=1B2M2Y8AsgTpgAmY7PhCfg%3d%3d&_t_q=svenska+finansiella+marknaden&_t_ tags=language%3asv%2csiteid%3af3366ed3-598f-4166-aa5a-45d5751e940b&_t_ip=130.237. 51.192&_t_hit.id=Riksbanken_Core_Models_Pages_ArticlePage/_9dda93fb-bb0c-4416-b259- 0de7471c3c43_sv&_t_hit.pos=2)

instead of paper-based systems such as checks and cash, and merchants as well as consumers—at least some segments—also saw advantages compared to the traditional payment services. The use of cards was low in the early stages but grew at a higher speed in the latter parts of the 1990s[4] and soon became a dominant part of retail payments. The number of terminals accepting card payments increased from around 25,000 in 1993 to almost 70,000 in 1996.[5] The central bank had also invested in and built an electronic system for clearing and settlement of payments—RIX—which provided additional incentives for banks to run electronic payment services. It should be noted however that many became disappointed with the relative slow growth of card payments in Sweden. The development was not as quick as in the neighboring Scandinavian countries.[6]

Interestingly the Swedish banks also tested an electronic form of cash in 1996. It was a cash card function that could be added to a traditional debit card based on the proton system that had been tried and used in Belgium. Money was stored on a chip—which then became a prepaid card—that could be used off-line and without

---

[4]Nyberg, L. and G. Guiborg. 2003. Kortbetalningar i Sverige. Penning- och valutapolitik 2/2003

[5]Sveriges Riksbank, 1997. Sveriges Riksbank. http://www.riksbank.se/sv/Press-och-publicerat/ Publicerat-fran-Riksbanken/Finansiell-stabilitet/Den-svenska-finansmarknaden/?all=1

[6]http://www.riksbank.se/en/Press-and-published/Press-Releases/2003/Nyberg-Overraskande-liten-anvandning-av-kontokort-i-Sverige-jamfort-med-vara-grannlander/

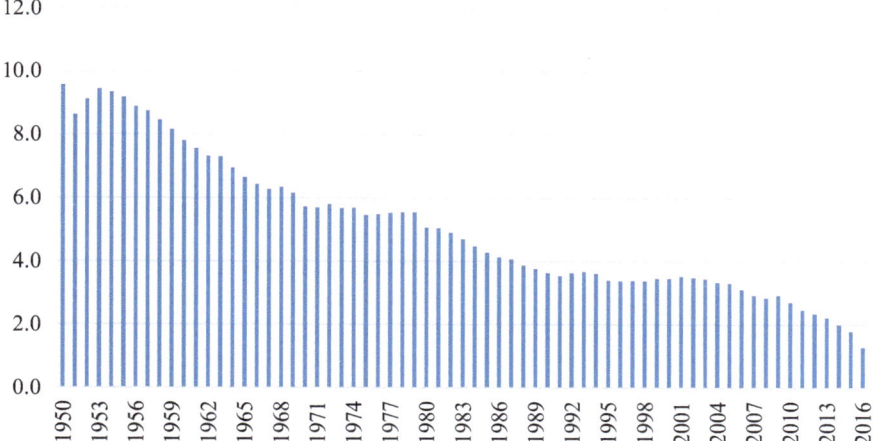

Fig. 4.2 Value of cash in circulation (SEK) as share of Swedish GDP (%) 1950–2016. Source: The Riksbank (https://www.riksbank.se/sv/press-och-publicerat/publikationer/om-finansiell-stabilitet/den-svenska-finansmarknaden/?_t_id=1B2M2Y8AsgTpgAmY7PhCfg%3d%3d&_t_q=svenska +finansiella+marknaden&_t_tags=language%3asv%2csiteid%3af3366ed3-598f-4166-aa5a-45d5751e940b&_t_ip=130.237.51.192&_t_hit.id=Riksbanken_Core_Models_Pages_ ArticlePage/_9dda93fb-bb0c-4416-b259-0de7471c3c43_sv&_t_hit.pos=2)

the need for identification and authentification. The benefits were less costly and faster transactions but the service was never really accepted and used by merchants, which meant it was soon closed down.[7]

As the new millennium—the year 2000—came closer, many in Sweden were enthusiastically engaged in creating a new society. Seductive concepts such as digitalization, a network economy, the new economy, e-commerce, broadband, and many others led to hopes of radical new technologies, business models, and companies that were to change Sweden and turn it into a completely new economy. Another concept that was talked about but really did not happen was mobile payments. The idea that we would be able to make payments through a mobile telephone was appealing and innovative.

The early 2000s saw a time where the hopes for new innovative payment services were high, but few services were launched in a successful way. Banks, telecom operators, and start-ups saw business potential in launching new payment services and intensified their efforts to develop such services but little happened. The time did launch these ideas, however, and became important in the sense that it laid the foundation for ambitions and business ideas that were to become realized 10–15 years later.

[7]Den svenska finansmarknaden 1997. Sveriges Riksbank. http://www.riksbank.se/sv/Press-och-publicerat/Publicerat-fran-Riksbanken/Finansiell-stabilitet/Den-svenska-finansmarknaden/?all=1

The next step was in hindsight somewhat surprising but became an important factor for the reduction of cash in Sweden. In the mid-2000s there was an increase in robberies of banks, merchants, and cash depots which led to new views on cash in the Swedish society. The number of reported robberies[8] in Sweden increased from 8590 in 2004 to 9398 in 2005—an increase with over 9% in 1 year. This peak stimulated increased lobbying campaigns against cash by unions in public transportation, banking, and merchants in the mid-2000s. They became active to reduce the use of cash from a work environment perspective since they simply did not want their members—the employees—to be exposed to robberies. Examples of this include *Tryggare rörelsen*[9] from the savings banks and *Kontantfritt.nu*[10] from the unions in the banking sector. Too many, too brutal, and too costly robberies of buses, banks, and merchants motivated unions to take action aiming at reducing the use of cash in the Swedish society.[11]

Yet another factor relates to the tax system. From 2004[12] and onward, the state introduced several different tax incentives aiming at, first, stimulating the economy via incentives for consumers and, second, turning sectors like construction and household services into transparent and taxpaying industries. Construction and household services to private consumers had a history of being based on nontaxed payments, i.e., part of the gray sector, which meant that suppliers of these services did not pay taxes but where they also often ended up in a poor situation when it came to accessing social benefits like unemployment benefits and pensions. There were additional tax incentives aiming to reduce the use of black money in the construction sector and for household services introduced in 2007. In 2008, the regulation stimulating tax payments for household services also started to include other services like cleaning and gardening.[13]

This meant that private persons could get tax reductions if they paid construction and/or household services for private houses. These incentives stimulated transparency in these sectors which in turn meant the cash payments were replaced by payments primarily via invoicing and therefore affected the use of cash in a negative way.

Another tax and tax evasion factor was the renewed efforts to force merchants to declare all their sales by introducing more strict control of the cash registers used by merchants. One background to these changes aims to make it more difficult for

---

[8]Rån, grovt rån. https://www.bra.se/brott-och-statistik/kriminalstatistik.html

[9]This was a movement aiming to make the society safer by reducing the use of cash. They run information and lobbying campaigns primarily aiming at convincing consumers to make card payments instead of using cash.

[10]This was an information and lobbying campaign from the unions aiming to make people see the benefits from a reduction of the use of cash.

[11]See, for instance, https://www.finansforbundet.se/om-oss/sa-tycker-vi/vara-asikter/kontantfritt-samhalle/

[12]http://www.regeringen.se/rattsdokument/proposition/2004/05/prop.-200304163/

[13]These services were called ROT (Renovering Ombyggnad Tillbyggnad) and RUT (Rengöring Underhåll och Tvätt).

cash-intensive industries to avoid paying taxes.[14] A new law was introduced in 2007 to realize these ambitions.[15] The tax authorities wanted to reduce the avoidance of paying taxes in restaurants, temporary merchants, and other merchant activities that traditionally were cash intensive.

The new laws stipulated that all cash registers must be impossible to manipulate and must provide possibilities for tax authorities to get information on sales, which in turn enabled tax authorities to control if they paid correct taxes or not. This made merchants gradually reduce the acceptance of cash and instead start to prefer card payments since these tend to be efficient, not too costly, and often liked by consumers.

In retrospect we see that the use of cash peaked in 2007 in Sweden when the nominal value of cash in circulation was at its highest level. Paradoxically it was at this point in time that the Riksbank made the decision to launch new bills and coins which was implemented in the period 2015–2017. The decision was at the time well-motivated by efforts to avoid counterfeit money and to make cash handling more efficient.

The Riksbank started to work on how the Swedish bills and coins could be modernized already in 2008.[16] The main reasons for this were that the bills and coins had not been changed for a long time and there was a need to improve efficiency, to reduce environmental impact, and to improve security. The central bank law was changed in 2009[17] which led to the introduction of new bills and coins in 2015–2017.[18] There had not been a fundamental change of Swedish cash for 30 years and it was basically time to do this. Somewhat paradoxically these discussions and aims came at the same time as the use of cash in Sweden were at its peak, which happened toward the end of 2007.

Another important event influencing the view of cash in Sweden occurred on September 23, 2009. In the morning of this day, the so-called helicopter robbery of a cash depot in Stockholm took place. This was a rigorously planned and executed robbery of a cash depot where they used a helicopter, explosives, and machine guns to steal 39 million SEK (around 4 million euros). The criminals put fake bombs to stop police helicopters to start and tools to stop police cars ("fotanglar"[19]), stolen cars, dumped the money, and finally landed the helicopter in a remote area and put it on fire. They got away with the money but one of them was caught.

---

[14]http://www.regeringen.se/rattsdokument/statens-offentliga-utredningar/2005/05/sou-200535/

[15]Lagen 2007:592 http://www.riksdagen.se/sv/dokument-lagar/dokument/svensk-forfattningssamling/lag-2007592-om-kassaregister-mm_sfs-2007-592

[16]http://www.riksbank.se/Upload/Dokument_riksbank/Kat_sedlar/mars_080307.pdf

[17]http://www.riksbank.se/Upload/Dokument_riksbank/Kat_sedlar/2010/Nr16_Riksdagsskrivelse.pdf

[18]http://www.riksbank.se/Documents/Protokollsbilagor/Direktionen/2012/probil_bilagaC_120529.pdf

[19]Google translate suggests that "fotangel" is translated into "caltrop" https://translate.google.se/?hl=sv#sv/en/fotangel

This spectacular robbery can be seen as the culmination of cash-related robberies in Sweden and led to a debate on whether or not it is a good idea to use cash in our society. I personally wrote an article[20] arguing that it is time to rethink the use of cash in Sweden and this article led to an emotional debate. A majority of the replies to my article argued strongly and emotionally that cash must be kept and that it was ludicrous to believe anything else.[21] Some agreed that there is a need to modernize the payment system, but the majority did not. It became very clear that no matter which opinion people had—wanting to keep cash or to get rid of it—the inner beliefs were strong and highly emotional.

This event illustrated the emotional ties to cash as one of the most important symbols of a nation-state and as a highly personal token of what a nation-state is. We confirmed this in a study done in August 2013[22] where we asked 1000 Swedes different questions related to how they make payments. One question was about their view on cash where 2/3 said they see that access to cash is a human right. A human right is comparable to access to food and water, free speech, a transparent and fair legal system, and so on. Interestingly, in the same study, the respondents said they used card payments more frequently than cash payments. It is evident that cash is a strong artefact and institution in our society.

As we know, money and payment services become successful if and when the users trust the system and its services. Cash has therefore a tradition of strong trust since the Swedish Government and the Riksbank—in combination with a lot of other factors—generally have been well equipped to make the Swedish crown a stable and reliable currency. This is especially true for the last 20 years. But it is of course not only the government and the Riksbank that are determining how much users trust the system.

In September 2012, the cash-in-transit service company *Panaxia* files for bankruptcy after having faced cash flow problems and illegally used clients' money to pay their own costs.[23] In this process, merchants—grocery stores, petrol stations, and others—lost a lot of money. Some over 100 MSEK. This led to a series of legal trials and the leaders of the company were found guilty and sentenced to imprisonment. The events seemingly led many merchants to question the cash system and to start considering not to accept cash anymore. Another effect from this case was that as Panaxia disappeared from the market, the competitive intensity decreased and fees for cash handling services tended to increase. This of course reduced the incentives for merchants to keep accepting cash.

It is of course a natural effect that cash primarily is used in the so-called proximity payments, i.e., where the payer and the payment receiver meet face-to-face. This

---

[20]Arvidsson, N. Vi behöver ett nytt betalsystem. Svenska Dagbladet, SvD.se, 7 oktober, 2009. https://www.svd.se/vi-behover-ett-nytt-betalsystem

[21]On a personal note, I was called things that cannot be printed in this book by people who had a strong interest to keep cash in Sweden.

[22]http://www.insightintelligence.se/sverige-betalar/det-kontantlosa-samhallet/

[23]http://sverigesradio.se/sida/avsnitt/538117?programid=2519

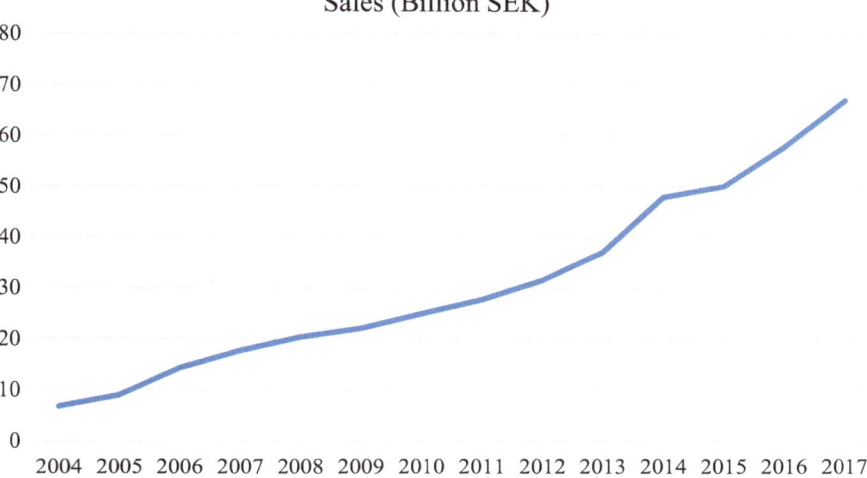

Fig. 4.3 E-commerce in Sweden 2004–2017. Source: E-barometern (2017) (https://www.iis.se/docs/e-barometern-arsrapport-2017.pdf)

means that as e-commerce grows and starts to replace purchases in physical stores, we should expect a decrease in the use of cash and a proportionate increase in the use of electronic payment services. E-commerce in Sweden has grown each year since 2004 and is currently almost 9% of all retail trade in Sweden (e-barometern, 2017) but continues to grow steadily in 2018 (e-barometern, 2018[24]). It is still not a major share of all retail trade, but the growth of e-commerce has definitely had an impact on the reduction of cash in the Swedish society.

Payments have increasingly become electronic and new actors are strong in the area of mobile payments and Internet payments—like Apple, Google, Paypal, Klarna, Seamless, iZettle, etc.—are also attracting young people being active on the Internet to start new purchasing behaviors. This has also stimulated a shift away from physical stores and cash to e-commerce and electronic payments (Fig. 4.3).

But we of course still need to make payments, and if the use of cash decreases, what do Swedes use instead? Well one answer came on December 12, 2012, at 00.12 am when a new mobile payment service called Swish is launched. This is an electronic payment service that initially enabled real-time transactions between consumers (person-to-person payments) without fees and therefore became a natural and efficient substitute to cash. The absence of fees and the real-time clearing makes it similar to cash in the sense that a transaction can be completed in 1 or 2 seconds. By connecting a mobile phone number to a bank account and connecting to a real-time clearing and settlement system, consumers were able to transfer money between bank accounts in a second or two. This meant that situations where people

---

[24]https://www.postnord.se/e-barometern

traditionally had used cash—splitting a bill in a restaurant, transferring money for purchases of gifts or tickets, buying a hot dog and a coffee at the sports arena, or even paying pocket money to kids—now could be handled via a mobile payment service.

After a slow start in 2013, this service gained users and today it has more than 6.5 million private users in a country were around 8.2 million are above the age of 15. This means that almost 80% of the potential users already are using it. And they are using it! During the fall of 2017, there were transactions with a value of around 8 billion SEK[25] per month which is about 10% of the value of card transactions each month.[26] In September 2018, there is a transaction of 17.8 billion SEK.[27] Swish has definitely made an impact when it comes to person-to-person payments in Sweden.

Another factor influencing the view of cash is the economic reports made by the Riksbank as well as the European Central Bank. The socioeconomic reports show that costs of cash are higher than costs of card payments. The social costs of a debit card payment were estimated to be 5.5 SEK, while the social costs of a cash payment were estimated to be 8.3 SEK (Segendorf & Jansson, 2012). The socioeconomic cost of cash payments were shown to be higher than those of debit card payments, which implies that a society may gain from reducing the use of cash. From a macroeconomic perspective, there are strong indications that a society would gain from replacing cash payments with debit card payments.

But there are of course also factors that lead to the conclusion to keep cash. As the reduction of cash continues from 2007 and onward, there are groups in the Swedish society that meet problems. Even if the majority of Swedes seems to adapt to the transition and actually also prefer electronic payment services, there are groups that prefer cash and have difficulties to accessing and depositing cash. The County Administration Board in Sweden[28] has been given the operative responsibility to study Swedes' access to basic payment services, i.e., access to cash, and their annual reports reveal problems for several groups in the Swedish society.

The latest report on access to basic payment services from the County Administration Board covering 2017 (Länsstyrelserna, 2017)[29] shows that problems related to poor access to basic payment services are a reality for many people. The report even see a risk of a digital divide where some groups in the society—for different reasons—cannot or will not be able to switch from using cash to using electronic payment services in a quick way and that therefore may risk facing serious difficulties in making payments. These problems are not only related to rural areas far away from the larger cities but can actually be seen in some area in all of the 24 counties in Sweden. It is primarily elderly people with physical and/or cognitive disabilities,

---

[25] https://www.getswish.se/

[26] The total value of POS terminal card transactions in 2016 was 997 billion SEK which gives a monthly average of around 83 billion SEK (http://www.riksbank.se/sv/Statistik/Betalningsstatistik/).

[27] https://www.getswish.se/

[28] Länsstyrelserna www.lst.se

[29] http://www.lansstyrelsen.se/Dalarna/SiteCollectionDocuments/Sv/Publikationer/Rapporter-2017/Grundlaggande-betaltjanster-2017.pdf

immigrants, as well as small merchants and organizations in rural areas that have problems when access to cash services deteriorates.

The problems with poor access to basic payment services have also led to a campaign aiming to keep cash or to slow down the decrease of cash in Sweden. There are constellations like "Kontantupproret"[30] (the Access to Cash Campaign) and several interest organizations for retired people like PRO and SPF[31] that perform lobbying with the aim to keep cash services in Sweden. "Kontantupproret" is led by Björn Eriksson and can be understood as an interest organization for the industry providing services related to protection and handling cash,[32] while PRO and SPF are consumer organizations focusing on elderly people. They have a shared interest in keeping cash handling services in Sweden.

In this movement, the former chief-of-police Björn Eriksson published a document called "Korten på Bordet[33]" (Eriksson, 2014[34]) in which he argues that cash payments must be protected and kept as a well-functioning payment service in Sweden. "Kontantupproret" has also acted to convince the government to take the issue of access to cash more seriously as many people are hurt when access to such services is reduced.[35] PRO has also acted in this matter by collecting names of people that want to keep cash in Sweden.[36] The lobbying have had an effect as one of the parties in the parliament—the Center Party—announced they will start working to keep cash in Sweden where, for instance, the role of the Riksbank in relation to cash can be changed,[37] which is discussed later in this book.

Yet another factor in this story is the introduction of new bills and coins in Sweden. As discussed above, this decision was taken in 2008 and implemented in 2015–2017. The change-over process started in October 2015 with new bills in the denomination of 20, 50, 200, and 1000 SEK. Interestingly, Sweden continued the use of the largest bill—the 1000 SEK bill—despite many arguing that it would be a good idea to stop issuing larger bills. It should be noted that 1000 SEK is

---

[30]The literal translation of "kontantupproret" is "cash rebellion" (http://www.kontantupproret.se/).

[31]Like Pensionärernas Riksorganisation (www.pro.se) and SPF (www.spfseniorerna.se)

[32]This includes companies like Loomis www.loomis.se and Nokas www.nokas.se.

[33]This translates into "Cards on the table."

[34]Interestingly, Björn Eriksson accuses the banks of driving an intensified lobbying campaign for getting rid of cash, while he in fact is doing the exact same thing – supported by companies providing services connected to cash handling – but with the aim to keep cash in the Swedish society.

[35]They have written (in Swedish): *Vår uppfattning är att Riksbanken och Kontantupproret tycks ha en samsyn i många frågor. Vi tycks dela verklighetsbeskrivningen om hur människor blir lidande av bankernas forcerade nedmontering av kontantsystemet. Vi uppfattar det också som att Riksbanken delar vår syn att det är problematiskt att bankväsendet har fått obegränsat inflytande över kontanthanteringen och att de berörda bankerna kan fortsätta att pressa fram sina positioner utan motstånd.* See http://www.kontantupproret.se/wp-content/uploads/2014/11/Skrivelse-till-Riksbanksfullma%CC%88ktige-fra%CC%8An-Kontantupproret-dec-2015.pdf

[36]http://www.pro.se/pension/Nyhetsarkiv/Kontanter-behovs/

[37]https://www.centerpartiet.se/lokal/fyrbodal/uddevalla/startsida/nyheter/nyheter/2017-01-28-centerpartiet-riksbanken-maste-se-till-att-kontanter-finns.html

approximately 100 euro or 120 USD which means it still has a rather low value if we compare to the largest bills in euro or USD. The old bills with denominations 20, 50, and 1000 SEK became invalid in June 2016. New bills denominated 100 and 500 SEK as well as coins denominated 1, 2, and 5 SEK came in October 2016. Finally, old bills denominated 100 and 500 SEK as well as coins denominated 1, 2, and 5 SEK became invalid in June 2017.

The introduction of new bills and coins does not seem to have had a positive effect on the use of cash, though. If anything, it seems to have had the opposite effect. One temporary effect is of course that all the old cash never returned to the central bank at all and therefore disappeared from the official statistics, but another seems to be that consumers and merchants seemingly have transformed their behavior and now instead are using electronic payment services instead of cash.

The value of all cash in circulation after the introduction of new bills and coins was around 50 billion SEK in October 2017[38] which is about 65% of the value in 2015 before the process started. The reduction only in 2017 is around 23%, and in the end of September 2018, the value of cash in circulation was 7% lower than the monthly average in 2017[39]! Paradoxically, it is not unlikely that instead of stimulating a renewed interest in cash, the new bills and coins led to a decreased interest in cash.

The decision to launch the new cash definitely made sense when it was taken as this was when the use of cash peaked. None at that time had foreseen the decline in the use of cash that has happened. As always, it is much easier to look backward and argue they were wrong than to look forward and rightly say how things should be done. A logical decision in 2008 given the information and knowledge at hand but that in retrospect may seem incorrect. And if you add that cash will still be around for a long time even if the use of it decreases, the decision to launch new bills and coins was justified.

There are several historic factors that can explain the reduction of cash in Sweden, but I will now turn to more recent factors.

References

E-barometern. (2017). *Årsrapport i samarbete mellan Svensk Digital Handel och HUI Research.*
E-barometern. (2018). *Årsrapport i samarbete mellan Svensk Digital Handel och HUI Research.*
Eriksson, B. (2014). *Korten på bordet—därför vill bankerna avskaffa kontanterna.*
Länsstyrelsen. (2017). *Bevakning av grundläggande betalningstjänster 2017.* Falun: Länsstyrelsen i Dalarna.
Nyberg, L., & Guiborg, G.. (2003). *Kortbetalningar i Sverige* (Penning-och valutapolitik 2/2003)

---

[38]http://www.riksbank.se/sv/Sedlar%2D%2Dmynt/Statistik/

[39]https://www.riksbank.se/sv/statistik/betalningar-sedlar-och-mynt/sedlar-och-mynt/

Segendorf, B., & Jansson, T. (2012). *The cost of consumer payments in Sweden* (Sveriges Riksbank Working Paper Series, no. 262).

Sveriges Riksbank. (1997). *Den svenska finansmarknaden*. Stockholm: Sveriges Riksbank.

Chapter 5
Cash in the Swedish Payment System Today

The use of cash in Sweden peaked in the end of 2007 and has been decreasing ever since. The decrease in 2017 has been remarkable when looking at value of cash in circulation. The value of Swedish cash in the end of October 2017 was 26% (!) lower than in the end of 2016. The decrease since the peak in 2007 is over 50%. And it should be noted that this decrease is mainly a result of how the so-called market—banks, merchants, and consumers—supplies and demands cash. The main action by the state—or rather the Riksbank—in this period is to have decided that new bills and coins are introduced in the period from 2015 to 2017. When studying (Table 5.1), it seems that the introduction of new bills and coins has had a negative effect on the use of cash where some of the decline is caused by the fact that all old cash is simply not returned to the central bank at all. There were cash with a total value of 8 billion SEK that had not been returned to the Riksbank by October 31, 2017, and thereby no longer were legal tender. This means that around a third of the decrease of cash in circulation was bills and coins that lost their status as legal tender in June 2017 but that nevertheless were not returned to the central bank. Despite this large temporary reduction due the new bills and coins, the decline was strong and critical.

In the latest report from CapGemini and BNP Paribas (World Payments Report, 2018), Sweden has actually passed the United States as the country where the most noncash transactions per capita are made. Sweden recorded 461.5 noncash transactions per inhabitant in 2016, whereas the former number one, the United States, recorded 459.6 transactions (World Payments Report, 2018, p. 8). This is yet another indicator showing the process toward a possibly cash-free society in Sweden is real and must be taken seriously.

We should note that the strong downward trend in the use of cash in Sweden is not representative for the globe.[1]

---

[1]See 2016 World Payments Report by CapGemini (page 11).

© The Author(s) 2019

N. Arvidsson, *Building a Cashless Society*, SpringerBriefs in Economics,
https://doi.org/10.1007/978-3-030-10689-8_5

Table 5.1 Value of cash in circulation (SEK; annual average based on last day of every month)

	2013	2014	2015	2016	2017	2018[a]
Nominal value (billion SEK)	88	80	77	65	57	54
Change from previous year (%)	−2.8	−9.1	−3.7	−15.6	−12.3	−5.3
Nominal value as share of GDP (%)	2.2	2.0	1.8	1.3	1.2	n.a.

Sources: The Riksbank and SCB (https://www.riksbank.se/en-gb/statistics/payments-notes-and-coins/notes-and-coins/)
[a]2018-10-31

Table 5.2 Average value of card payments in Sweden (SEK)

	2007	2008	2009	2010	2011	2012	2013	2014	2015	2016
Average value of card payments in Sweden (SEK)	464	435	420	403	411	388	375	374	322	316

Sources: The Riksbank and SCB

The total number of retail payment is of course not decreasing, quite the contrary. But cash payments are being replaced primarily by card payments and mobile payment services like Swish. Card payments are used for lower and lower values and therefore more frequently and covering more value (Table 5.2). Now we also see that the launch of contactless cards in Sweden drive the use of cards even further. Contactless cards came late to Sweden, but the industry now has ambitious plans. The plan for launching contactless cards in Sweden was developed by the Contactless Forum,[2] which was a forum for collaboration between card companies, banks, and technology providers with the aim to realize a system for contactless card payments in Sweden.

Their aim was that 54% of cards and 46% of POS-terminals should be a reality by the end of 2017,[3] which were targets that were reached. Contactless card payments are interesting since they, first, constitute a direct substitute to cash as the payment process is quick and easy, and, second, they are likely to strengthen the use of mobile payment services by realizing an infrastructure and start changing our behavior when making payments. The introduction of contactless cards drove installment of NFC-readers in stores which will make the transition into mobile payments via NFC easier.

The increase of e-commerce over purchases in physical stores also stimulates card payments and other electronic forms of payment over cash payments. Finally, Swish payments have grown significantly and become an important substitution to cash (Tables 5.3 and 5.4).

---

[2]http://contactless.se/om-contactless-forum/

[3]It should be noted that this forum later was replaced by Card Payments Sweden (CPS) (http://contactless.se/bild-ett/).

Table 5.3 Growth of Swish 2012–2017

	2012	2013	2014	2015	2016	2017
Private users (millions)	0.09	0.7	2.1	3.8	5.1	6.1
Transactions private users (billion SEK)	0.02	1.9	10.9	41.4	87.1	135.4
Retail and organizational users (thousands)	Not in use	Not in use	10	49	100	147
Transactions retail and organizational user (billion SEK)	Not in use	Not in use	0.06	0.8	4.5	14.7

Source: www.getswish.se

Table 5.4 The use of Swish in September 2018

	Number of users (millions)	Payments (millions)	Value of transactions (billion SEK)	Average value per transaction (SEK)	Growth of users last year (%)	Growth of value of transactions last year (%)
Private	6.6	25.5	15.2	597	12	+29
Business	0.17	4.4	1.5	340	31	+55
Retailers	0.03	4.8	1.1	237	124	+137
Total	6.8	34.7	17.8	515	13	+35

Source: www.getswish.se

Reference

World Payments Report 2018 by CapGemini and BNP Paribas.

Chapter 6
Understanding the Process Toward a Cashless Society

Cash Payments: A Socio-technical System

One way of understanding transformation of industries and technologies is to apply a so-called socio-technical analysis, which is based on the prerequisite that it is only by understanding the interplay between several critical factors that makes it possible to grasp how and why transformation happens. We cannot study technological innovation in isolation if we want to understand change. Nor can we study organizational or individual behavior or factors such as politics, culture, laws, environmental aspects, or internationalization in isolation. Complex patterns of transformation are ideally studied by acknowledging this complexity while at the same time trying to reduce this complexity into understandable patterns and structures.

I will therefore use a well-known approach to structure my analysis of the transformation of cash-based payment services in Sweden, i.e., the definition of a socio-technical systems where it is linkages between critical elements and resources—such as technologies, capital, knowledge, culture, and others—that will decide the function and change of the system (Geels, 2004, p. 900). My analysis focuses on cash-based payments in Sweden today and will use Geels' model (2004) to structure my analysis and discussion.

This approach views the payment system as a sectoral innovation system where emphasis is put on:

> ...the structure of the system in terms of products, agents, knowledge and technologies and on its dynamics and transformation. In broader terms, one could say that a sectoral system is a collective emergent outcome of the interaction and co-evolution of its various elements (Malerba, 2002, p. 251)

The payment system development is understood to be driven by a collection of organizations, people, competences, and interests that collaborate and compete in different constellations, which also may change over time. My approach is in line with the call by Moulaert and Sekia (2003) and Martin and Sunley (2003) for models

© The Author(s) 2019
N. Arvidsson, *Building a Cashless Society*, SpringerBriefs in Economics,
https://doi.org/10.1007/978-3-030-10689-8_6

of innovation that addresses dynamics and evolutionary dimensions of innovation processes.

I do not see the transformation as possibly created by one specific type of actor—such as commercial banks, cash-in-transit service companies, merchants, or consumers—it is rather the combination of these and other actors' action that constitute change or perhaps lack of change.

The choice of this theoretical approach (Geels, 2004; Malerba, 2002) is motivated by the basic characteristics of the payment industry. Cash payments are characterized by strong regulation and governmental policy regimes, technology regimes[1] (Dosi, 1982) related to payment services, a defined user and market regime both in terms payees and payers, a strong sociocultural regime related to the view of cash in a market economy,[2] as well as a science regime related to research and development in the payment industry. By deploying this perspective I will also be able to complement Rogoff's (2016) top-down and macroeconomic analysis of the use of cash in a market economy.

I have in other studies (Arvidsson, 2014a, 2014b, 2016, 2018a, 2018b; Arvidsson, Hedman, & Segendorf, 2018) shown how a number of different sociotechnical factors influence the use of cash in the Swedish society. Here are some of the most important ones.

A starting point for an analysis of a service like cash is of course to understand what the government and the law says about this service. Interestingly, the Government of Sweden states that access to basic payment services, i.e., cash, should be provided to everyone in the society—consumers as well as organizations—but it is only the responsibility of the state to provide such services if the market fails to do so.[3] The main role of the government—and the Riksbank—is then to oversee that such services are provided by the market. This has made the market for cash decentralized and market-driven which is yet another factor explaining the reduction of cash in Sweden.

The decentralized and market-driven features are evident in the process of producing and transporting cash in the Swedish economy. The Riksbank does not govern how much cash that is in circulation in Sweden; this is decided by demand from the users of cash, i.e., banks, merchants, and primarily the consumers. The Riksbank provides the volume of cash that the public needs. The main responsibility of the Riksbank is to provide Sweden with banknotes and coins by issuing banknotes and coins, destroying worn-out banknotes and coins, and redeeming invalid

---

[1]A technology regime is a dominating technological system in a given time period in a given industry. We see this in many industries, and when discussing payments, I would argue that cash in its current form, i.e., central bank money issued in paper and coins, is a so-called dominant design of cash in a technological regime.

[2]By this I mean the former notion that issuing cash could be used to finance the state via seignorage and that it could be used as a governmental instrument to influence and manage financial markets via interest rates.

[3]http://www.regeringen.se/artiklar/2016/08/ansvarsfordelning-for-kontanthantering/

banknotes.[4] Printing cash (SEK) has been outsourced to private companies,[5] and storing as well as transporting cash is done by Bankernas Depå AB (BDB), which is owned by the largest banks, and by private companies like Loomis and Nokas. Then ATMs, banks, and merchants provide access to cash for private persons. This decentralized, operative, and market-driven structure is also complemented by the legal framework governing the use of cash.

One fundamental factor is the legal constitution in Sweden that actually allows a merchant to say: "I do not accept cash." As far as I know, this legal setup is unique to Sweden and one important reason why the use of cash is decreasing rapidly. The central bank law states that cash is legal tender,[6] but this can be set aside if a merchant and her customer enter an agreement that cash is not a viable payment option in a particular store. Commercial law[7] states that two parties—a merchant and a consumer or a bank and a consumer—can enter an agreement where the central bank law is set aside. This agreement can be written or oral. Thus, if a merchant has a sign saying that cash is not accepted and a customer enters this store and wants to buy something, the customer is seen to have entered a contractual agreement not to use cash. In practical terms, cash is not legal tender for privately owned businesses running a merchant store.[8]

You can expect signs saying a store will not accept cash in Sweden which is very different from what you may see in Tokyo where stores in fact may accept nothing but cash (Fig. 6.1).

New technological solutions or payment services that have a similar functionality to cash can therefore substitute cash in payment situations where cash used to be the main service that was used. This includes a service like Swish (Arvidsson, 2015) that can replace cash in person-to-person payments and a service like iZettle that enabled mobile point-of-sale (POS) terminals where card payments could replace cash payments in situations like temporary stands selling fruits and vegetables, street vendors, small merchants, and small kiosks at sports arenas. The combination of a legal possibility and technological innovations made it rather easy for merchants to consider to stop accepting cash.

Another factor influencing the use of cash is the values and emotions connected to cash that I touched upon before. Unions in banking, merchant industries, and public transportation see cash as a root to problems since several cash-related robberies including the hyped helicopter robbery took place in the mid-2000s, which of course

---

[4]http://www.regeringen.se/artiklar/2016/08/ansvarsfordelning-for-kontanthantering/

[5]Production of Swedish cash was for a long time outsourced to Crane Currency, but recently this was terminated https://www.riksbank.se/globalassets/media/nyheter%2D%2Dpressmeddelanden/pressmeddelanden/2018/the-riksbank-gives-notice-to-terminate-contract-with-crane-ab.pdf

[6]Lagen (1988:1385) om Sveriges riksbank i dess lydelse den 1 juli 2012.

[7]Avtalsrätten.

[8]This situation has not really been tested in court; however, but it depicts how merchants and their customer behave today. There is a court ruling saying that publically funded services and organizations—such as a health care provider—must accept cash if the customer wants to pay in cash. See Ruling by Kammarrätten in Sundsvall June 5, 2013, in case number 852-12.

Fig. 6.1 Signs you may see in Swedish stores (on top) and a sign you may see in Japanese stores (to the bottom). Source: Author's own illustration

hurt their members—the employees in these industries. The cash-in-transit service companies in combination with elderly instead see cash as necessary and helpful services enabling all consumers to make payments and all merchants to receive payments in a convenient way. Other groups like tech nerds and youngster are simply not interested in cash since electronic payment services and especially mobile payments or even virtual currencies are more convenient and definitely more intriguing. All of them are of course right—from their perspective!

We all know how difficult it is to change an old habit, and this is definitely true when it comes to how we make payments. Even if we see a transition from cash payments to electronic payments in Sweden, we also see that some groups have ingrown habits of using cash that perhaps never will change. This is especially true for elderly that have used cash in all their lives and are likely to continue doing it as long as they will make payments. There are in other words also factors that work in the direction of keeping cash.

The Access to Cash Campaign[9] is another force that works to stop the decreased use of cash. Their argument is that some groups in society depend on cash, and it is the obligation of the state—and actors like banks—to supply services that enable depositing and withdrawing cash. The annual reports from *Länsstyrelserna* give these arguments strong support. There is an increasing share of people—elderly, people with physical and/cognitive disabilities and immigrants—that have problems if cash cannot be used. In a state like Sweden with its tradition of taking care of and supporting weaker citizens, these problems cannot—and should not—be left unattended.[10]

It is also important to see the commercial interests underlying the transition from cash to electronic payment services. There are some industries—cash-in-transit service companies like Loomis and Nokas, cash producers like Crane Currency, guard service providers like Securitas and G4S, as well as providers of systems for cash handling like Siemens and BANQIT—that have a business interest related to the existence of cash. Other industries—automated clearing houses like Bankgirot; banks like Swedbank and Klarna;[11] Fintech companies like Betalo, Tink, and Payair; card providers like Visa and Mastercard; telecom companies as Apple, Samsung, Telia, and Tre; social media companies like Google and Facebook; e-commerce companies like Alibaba and Amazon, as well as providers of hardware and software solutions for electronic payments—have business interests in replacing cash payments with electronic payments. Merchants—payment receivers—have an interest in low fees and high value for these services as well as not relying too heavily on one specific payment service. Consumers—payers—have basic needs to be able to receive and make payments in as inexpensive, quick, effortless, and fun ways as possible. In addition, governments and central banks have a need for secure, reliable, and efficient payment systems to enable markets to operate as effectively as possible. This variety of interests makes the evolution of the payment system an interesting but complex process.

We can also make a somewhat deeper analysis of the business interest of banks in connection to cash. When banks started to sell bank accounts in the 1960s to consumers and were able to convince employers of the benefits from paying wages and salaries into bank accounts instead of via cash, this was as a win-win situation for all that were involved. But the unions had a strong demand—the banks should not be able to issue fees to consumers for accessing their wages and salaries. Access to this money should not have a price tag on it. This led to a situation where

---

[9]www.kontantupproret.se

[10]Then, we could of course have a discussion of how to solve these problems. Cash is not the only solution and perhaps not always the best solution for these groups. Prepaid contactless cards without the need for PIN codes for low-value payments could, for instance, be an alternative solution.

[11]http://www.fi.se/contentassets/7c8169d883f643f290632afe70989af7/bank-tillsynsrapport-2017ny.pdf

Swedish banks could not make a profit on cash-based services as such. They needed to find other ways to gain revenues that could pay for these services, and they did.

Annual fees for access to cards and interchange fees to merchants meant that the card payment business could pay the cash handling (and still leave a nice profit!). This tradition means that banks today have no commercial interest to keep supplying cash handling services—it is just costly and there are no cross-selling opportunities related to cash—and we have seen the effects from this. The share of bank retail offices that provide cash handling services is now below 50% (Länsstyrelserna, 2016).

Another factor that is important to take into consideration concerns the nature of payment services. A payment service—like other infrastructure services as telecommunication and electricity—benefits from having many suppliers and many users connected to the same technological platform. A payment service must realize network effects and interoperability (Economides, 1996; Hagiu & Wright, 2015) to become valuable for both payers and payees (i.e., payment receivers). This depends on the number of users—in each side—in the system.

To build a new payment, service becomes a classical chicken-and-the-egg problem where you need both at the same. If there are not many payment receivers, stores, the payers, consumers, will not be attracted to the service and vice versa. The open four-party card payment systems from VISA and Mastercard are good examples of such systems. You can use your card from a—let's say—Swedish bank when you want to make a payment in Chiang Mai, Thailand, or when you want to buy from an international e-commerce site.

I would even argue that the interoperability of card payment systems is their main competitive edge in this transition of payment systems. It is of course not a bad thing to have. VISA and Mastercard show strong profits year by year.[12] But this is not what I had planned to write in this paragraph. I got sidetracked by the enormous profitability in the payment industry, which of course is one reason why there are so many Fintech companies that want to enter this industry! There are a lot of potential dollars and euros in the payment industry that Fintech companies want to get their hands on.

But back to the plan to write that a new payment service that wants to be established must be able to overcome this chicken-and-the-egg problem. They need to attract large number of payers and payment receivers at the same time.[13] Cash in Sweden is now facing the opposite challenge—to keep as many payment receivers and payers as possible in the system. Fewer merchants accept cash, fewer banks offer cash handling services, and fewer consumers prefer cash, which in the end means reduced interoperability of cash and reduced value of the entire network for cash-based system! The cash-based system in Sweden is in situation with a

---

[12]https://www.reuters.com/article/us-visa-results/visas-profit-revenue-tops-estimates-on-payment-volume-growth-idUSKBN15H2S0

[13]As shown by Apanasevic (2018), there are several that have tried and failed.

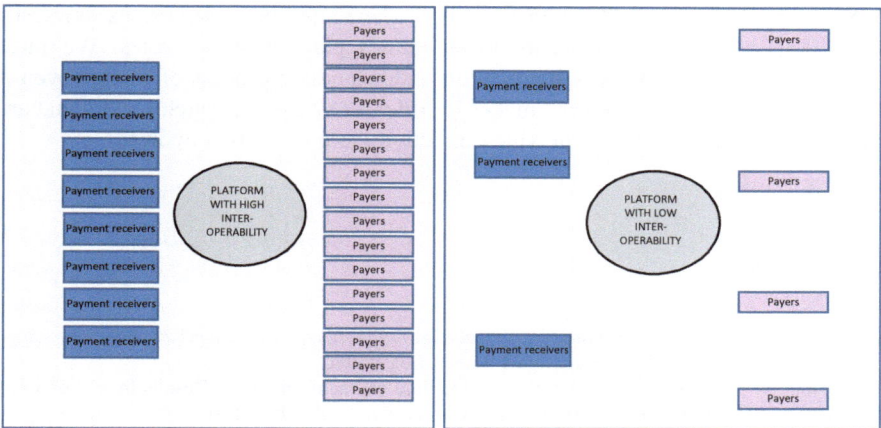

Fig. 6.2 From high to low interoperability for cash payment services. Source: Author's own illustration

decreasing interoperability and reduced network effects which has initiated a vicious circle that even may be self-reinforcing (Fig. 6.2).

I understand the process leading to a reduction of the network value—interoperability of cash—can be comparted to what Gladwell (2006)[14] defines as a "tipping point." This is a point at which a slow gradual decline leads to a situation where more and more payers as well as payees stop using or accepting cash since the network value is too low in relation to the costs of continuing to use or accept cash. The process becomes contagious, and actors start to imitate each other—sometimes without even thinking about it.

Tipping point:

> that magic moment when ideas, trends and social behavior cross a threshold, tip and spread like wildfire (Malcolm Gladwell[15])

Looking retrospectively the process toward a possible tipping point for cash in Sweden started after the cash peak in 2007 and has gradually gained force since then. Arguably, the exchange of bills and coins in Sweden in 2015–2017 became the time when this tipping point hit Sweden with its full force. Not that the introduction of new cash drove this process—it just happened to occur at the same time. And the downturn is not over yet. We see that 97% of merchants in Sweden still accept cash, but we also see that about 1/4 of them will stop accepting cash by 2020 and another 1/4 by 2025 (Arvidsson et al., 2018). The process has seemingly tipped and is now hitting Sweden with its full force.

---

[14]See the discussion of tipping points by Malcolm Gladwell in the book *The Tipping Point: How Little Things Can Make a Big Difference* (2006).

[15]Gladwell, M. (2006). *The Tipping Point: How Little Things Can Make a Big Difference*.

To sum up, it is a complex transformation where laws, politics, business interests, technologies, values, habits, and power games play important roles. We must acknowledge this complexity if we are to understand the process of change even if the complexity at the same time makes it difficult to pinpoint which factors that are the most important ones and in which direction the process will evolve.

References

Apanasevic, T. (2018). *Opportunities and challenges of mobile payment services: The perspective of service providers.* Diss., Kungliga Tekniska högskolan.

Arvidsson, N. (2014a). Consumer attitudes on mobile payment services – Results from a proof of concept test. *International Journal of Bank Marketing, 32*(2), 150–170.

Arvidsson, N. (2014b). A study of turbulence in the Swedish payment system – Is there a way forward? *Foresight, 16*(5), 462–482.

Arvidsson, N. (2015). Emergence of an ICT-based disruptive mobile payment service. In E. Giertz, A. Rickne, & P. Rouvinen (Eds.), *Small and beautiful – The ICT success of Finland & Sweden.* VINNOVA Analysis, VA 2015:06 (Chap. 15, pp. 200–208).

Arvidsson, N. (2016). *Framväxten av mobila, elektroniska betalningstjänster i Sverige – En studie av förändring inom betalsystemet* (Konkurrensverket, Uppdragsforskningsrapport 2016:4).

Arvidsson, N. (2018a). The future of cash. In R. Teigland, S. Siri, A. Larsson, A. Moreno Puertas, & C. Ingram Bogusz (Eds.), *The rise and development of Fintech – Accounts of disruption from Sweden and beyond* (Chap. 4, pp. 85–98). Routledge: Routledge International Studies in Money and Banking. London: Taylor & Francis Group.

Arvidsson, N. (2018b). The payment landscape in Sweden. In R. Teigland, S. Siri, A. Larsson, A. Moreno Puertas, & C. Ingram Bogusz (Eds.), *The rise and development of Fintech – Accounts of disruption from Sweden and beyond* (Chap. 13, pp. 238–252). Routledge: Routledge International Studies in Money and Banking. London: Taylor & Francis Group.

Arvidsson, N., Hedman, J., & Segendorf, B. (2018). *När slutar svenska handlare acceptera kontanter?* (Handelsrådet, Forskningsrapport 2018:1).

Dosi, G. (1982). Technological paradigms and technological trajectories – A suggested interpretation of the determinants and directions of technical change. *Research Policy, 11*, 147–162.

Economides, N. (1996). The economics of networks. *International Journal of Industrial Organization, 14*(6), 673–699.

Geels, F. W. (2004). From sectoral systems of innovation to socio-technical systems: Insights about dynamics and change from sociology and institutional theory. *Research Policy, 33*(6–7), 897–920.

Gladwell, M. (2006). *The tipping point: How little things can make a big difference.* New York: Little, Brown and Company.

Hagiu, A., & Wright, J. (2015). Multi-sided platforms. *International Journal of Industrial Organization, 43*(2015), 162–174.

Länsstyrelserna. (2016). *Bevakning av grundläggande betalningstjänster 2016.* Falun: Länsstyrelsen i Dalarna.

Malerba, F. (2002). Sectoral systems of innovation and production. *Research Policy, 31*(2), 247–264.

Martin, R., & Sunley, P. (2003). Deconstructing clusters: Chaotic concept or policy panacea? *Journal of Economic Geography, 3*(1), 5–35.

Moulaert, F., & Sekia, F. (2003). Territorial innovation models: A critical survey. *Regional Studies, 37*(3), 289–302.

Rogoff, K. S. (2016). *The curse of cash*. Princeton, NJ: Princeton University Press.

World Payments Report 2016 by CapGemini.

Chapter 7
Stories from a Close to Cash-Free Society

I have discussed, explained, and shown many different aspects and dimensions related to a transformation toward a cash-free society, but I believe something is missing. The complexity of this change process cannot be fully understood if we do not listen to some of the voices of those most severely influenced by the transition. What do people think about this, and how do they live their lives in Sweden today? Then I do not mean people in general, but rather, how do people make payments and how do they receive money? The data and numbers presented in previous chapters tend to refer to a general image of what is happening, but how do people actually handle payments? This cannot be seen in numbers but needs stories. Here are stories that reflect different aspects of living in a close to cash-free society.

The General Story of Sweden

Sweden is a rather small country with 10 million people, but it is large in terms of geographic size. The geographic size of Sweden is around 447,000 square kilometers or 174,000 square miles.[1, 2] This means the country is geographically larger than Japan, Germany, Italy, Iraq, the United Kingdom, Paraguay, and Zimbabwe. Just to mention some. We are about the same size as Uzbekistan.[3] But if you compare how many people that live in each of these countries, another picture becomes clear. The geographic distance between people is huge in Sweden which makes it difficult to supply cash handling services to all at a decent price.

---

[1]From here on I will abbreviate a square kilometer with km^2.

[2]There are about 2.59 square kilometers to 1 square mile.

[3]http://www.nationmaster.com/country-info/stats/Geography/Land-area/Square-miles

© The Author(s) 2019
N. Arvidsson, *Building a Cashless Society*, SpringerBriefs in Economics,
https://doi.org/10.1007/978-3-030-10689-8_7

Population density in Sweden, if compared to countries with similar economic development,[4] is 24 per km^2; in Germany, it is 236 per km^2; in the United Kingdom, it is 274 per km^2; and in Japan, it is 350 per km^2. It is definitely more expensive—per transaction—to supply cash handling services to everyone in Sweden than it is in cash-intensive countries like Germany and Japan. This is one explanation as to why cash handling services in remote parts of Sweden are shut down. Too few users and large geographical distances between payers, payees on the one hand, and ATMs and cash depots on the other make the equation clear. People meet problems as cash handling services become expensive and/or less accessible if they do not want to—or cannot—use and/or accept electronic payment services. And retailers face increasing difficulties and costs to bank their money at the end of the day.

The County Administrative Boards of Sweden[5] have the responsibility to observe, report on, and manage a selection of governmental activities and concerns in different parts of Sweden. The country is currently divided into 21 counties, and there is a county administration in each county. One of their responsibilities is to report on peoples' and organizations' access to basic payment services, i.e., cash. They report on this each year, and their latest report concluded that access to basic payment services is not improving and sometimes even deteriorating. I have discussed this earlier, but I want to add some information on a more concrete level here.

The report for 2017 (Länsstyrelserna, 2017) shows that 11 out of 21 counties report that access to basic payment services for elderly is not acceptable, and 8 counties report that it has deteriorated compared to 2016 (Länsstyrelserna, 2017, p. 14). It also reports that 13 out of 21 counties see that access to basic payment services for people with disabilities is not acceptable, and 8 counties report that it has deteriorated compared to 2016 (ibid).

Problems are also seen for immigrants and smaller organizations. When studying small organizations, 15 out of 21 counties report that access to basic payment services for organizations is not acceptable (Länsstyrelserna, 2017, p. 19). Investments in digital infrastructure, new payment services, and support from the government can help remedy some of the negative effects, but problems are not to be ignored and not easily solved. Even if a majority of Swedes and Swedish organizations and companies welcome the growth of electronic payment services, there is a large group of people and organizations that do not.

But how does this transformation affect people and organizations that traditionally have been depending on cash? Here are some stories.

---

[4]https://esa.un.org/unpd/wpp/Publications/Files/WPP2017_Wallchart.pdf
[5]http://www.lansstyrelsen.se/Sv/Pages/default.aspx

Situation Stockholm[6]: Empowering Homeless People

The social development in Sweden during the 1980s and 1990s led to a number of factors making life increasingly problematic for drug addicts, alcoholics, mentally disorderly people, and others that were living in the outskirts of society. They simply had problems to find a place to live and a basic income to pay the rent. Several events led to this situation including a liberalization of the Swedish economy during the 1980s that led to a more market-driven system for apartments and rents; a financial—or rather real estate—crash in the early 1990s that slowed down the economy[7]; a psychiatric reform[8] in the mid-1990s that transferred people from psychiatric care facilities to the streets; and generally more liberal labor market that made it more difficult for these groups to find and keep a job. All in all, people that previously had had problems to live in the Swedish society found it increasingly difficult to do this in the 1990s.

This situation led some people to react and take initiatives to help those that suffered the most from these events. Malin Lindfors Speace[9] and a few others, among them the editor in chief Ulf Stolt, decided to help in a somewhat different way. Instead of donating money or pushing politicians, companies, or other people to act and provide money, Malin believed that a person—any person—is best helped when he or she sees a purpose in life and can personally act to fulfill this purpose. Providing shelters and food to homeless people is good, but it will not solve the problem for these people. It is only when people are empowered to solve their own, personal problems that sustainable and fundamental change is realized.

The organization Situation Stockholm was then created with the ambition to provide opportunities for people to help themselves, which is very different from helping marginalized people by providing money, food, and shelter, says Jenny Lindroth who is head of the social operations of Situation Stockholm.

Vi erbjuder sysselsättning, inte pysselsättning[10] says Jenny Lindroth.

The aim is not to minimize the harm these persons may do to society or—more likely—to themselves but instead to empower them to take control of their lives and thereby build a better future. And the tool is not to prohibit things and control the actions of people. It is instead based on the idea that people are the best tools for their

---

[6]http://www.situationsthlm.se/

[7]See: Perbo, U. (1999). Varför fick Sverige en depression i början av 90-talet. Ekonomisk Debatt 1999, årg 27, nr 6, s.325–333 (http://www.ne.su.se/ed/pdf/27-6-up.pdf).

[8]This was based on an investigation done by the Swedish parliament in the beginning of the 1990s (Psykiatriutredningen, SOU 1992:73).

[9]https://www.svd.se/det-maste-finnas-ett-syfte

[10]This is a Swedish pun that is difficult to translate into English but that essentially means we offer employment, not meaningless activities that just aim to keep people busy. The Swedish version is of course rather funny and to the point (trust me!) since the words only differ in terms of one letter.

own change if good circumstances are provided, and they build their own inner drive to achieve change.

The organization offers their target groups, i.e., homeless, ex-homeless, and other people in social distress, an opportunity to build their private economy, to achieve control of their lives, and to stop being lured into crimes. These people often have problems with drug abuse and addiction as well as social and psychological problems. The purpose is to provide an organized life and structure, well-earned money, a road away from drug abuse, as well as education and general support. Situation Stockholm offers training and help aiming to enable the homeless people to create a decent life in the Swedish society. The overall aim is to rehabilitate people in need via work and training.

The main tool for achieving their purpose is a magazine called Situation Stockholm that is sold by the persons the organization aims to help. A homeless person can contact the organization and say that he or she wants to start selling their magazine in the streets of Stockholm. The vendors need to follow a few and simple rules mainly focusing on acting proper when selling the magazines and have a license provided by Situation Stockholm. They also need to sign a contract including a promise to follow the rules set up by the organization, and if they fail to follow these rules, they may lose their license to sell the magazine.

Why selling a magazine you may wonder. Could they not sell anything—soft drinks, candy, lottery tickets, or something else—that people want to buy? Well, the answer is simple. The laws governing the free media and the "free word" in Sweden mean that it is possible to sell media products—like magazines—on the streets without special permits. Their magazine is writing about social issues and therefore qualifies as free media.

How does it work? A vendor first needs to get the license and permit to sell the magazine as well as to follow the rules set up by Situation Stockholm. Then they buy magazines from the organization and pay 25 Swedish crowns per magazine. Yes, they need to pay for each magazine before they sell them. This means the vendors need to plan their financial situation and make sure they have enough money to buy—invest in—new magazines when the old ones are sold. This is an incentive to save money and plan for the future.

Thereafter they are given spots in Stockholm where they can sell the magazines. The geographical spots are issued by Situation Stockholm to avoid people fighting over the best spots. The magazines are then sold for the price of 50 crowns per magazine. A vendor earns 25 crowns per magazine—a 50% margin which is probably twice as much as the industry norm.

And now you probably wonder why a book about cashlessness writes about homeless people selling magazines in Stockholm. It is because they were among the first in Stockholm to adopt the new innovative noncash payment services that had been developed. According to standard innovation diffusion theories (Rogers, 2010; Wiefels & Moore, 2002), it should be the tech freaks and nerds that are the first to adopt innovative, technologically advanced services. It should be students at our university—the Royal Institute of Technology—or hackers and programmers never seeing daylight and surviving on caffeine drinks and burgers. Here we instead have a

Fig. 7.1 The magazine Situation Stockholm in April and July 2018. Source: https://www.situationsthlm.se/tidningsarkiv/

story of how homeless people are among the first to start accepting mobile payment services in Sweden! Quite remarkable.

When Homeless People Taught Stockholm to Use Mobile Payments

The first issue of the magazine called Situation Stockholm was sold in August 1995, and a new issue has been sold every month since then (Fig. 7.1). The current number of magazines sold is around 20,000 per month which generate around 1.1 million crowns per month,[11] out of which the vendors get half, and there are around 300 active vendors each year. The money they earn may not be enough to pay the rent, food, and clothing, but it is definitely enough to enable these people to start having control of their lives. Having 120 crowns per day, a free breakfast provided by Situation Stockholm, a purpose and aim, access to training, and a social environment stimulating good behavior make a dramatic difference for people previously without home and hope.

The sales of Situation Stockholm had been increasing since the start in 1995, but in 2012, there were indications of a new problem. The vendors reported that potential buyers more and more often said they wanted to buy the magazine but that they did not carry cash in their pockets. Vendors were asked if they accepted card payments which they did not do at this time. These events were signs of the

---

[11]This is about 131,000 USD or 106,000 Euro.

decline of cash in Sweden where Stockholm was taking the lead in using less and less cash. The organization faces a new problem as vendors only accepted cash and many people did not carry cash in their wallets anymore.

So, what needed to be done?

The organization understood that in order to keep up sales, they needed to accept other forms of payments than cash. They therefore looked for solutions and first tested a voucher system that did not work. Then they tested a SMS payment solution in 2013 that was provided by telecom operators under the name of WyWallet.[12] This service helped sales, but there were also problems related to changed legislation which affected the providers[13] as well as the fact that vendors had to be provided with mobile phones, which in itself meant challenges for the organization. Some vendors simply sold the phones, used them for illegal or immoral purposes, or sometimes accidentally dropped them leading to malfunctioning phones. And, these payment services were rather costly. Despite these new challenges and set-backs, the tests had shown that the decision to offer noncash payment services was a good decision.

And it actually also made many Stockholmers aware of a new payment service landscape where other services than cash could be used in situations where cash previously had been "the King." The vendors of Situation Stockholm can be said to have taught many people in Stockholm their first lessons in how to use mobile payment services.

The next step was to contact one of the growing Swedish Fintech companies called iZettle[14] that was providing mobile point-of-sale terminals for card payments[15] which could mean that if vendors had smartphones and a dongle that was connected to the phone, they could accept card payments. And since almost every Swede has a debit or credit card, this could be a perfect solution. And it was. Even if there were still problems since the vendors are needed to be educated to use these somewhat complicated services and to start carry smartphones and other equipment that constantly needed to be charged, the solution proved helpful. Situation Stockholm vendors now became among the first magazine vendors to accept card payments in the streets!

> This also made our people more technologically advanced than many of the small coffee shops and merchants next door to our vendors. Our vendors became aware—and rightly proud—of offering advanced payment options when the coffee shop still only accepted cash and card payments. Their self-esteem grew and our basic aim behind our activities proved itself, say Jenny Lindroth.

---

[12]http://wywallet.se/

[13]The first payment service directive from the European Union meant new demands on actors providing payment services which forced any provider – including telecom operators – to follow more strict regulations and procedures.

[14]www.izettle.com. It should be noted that iZettle recently was acquired by PayPal for a stunning 2.2 billion USD (https://www.bbc.com/news/business-44161814).

[15]This is similar to the services provided by Square in the United States. https://squareup.com/

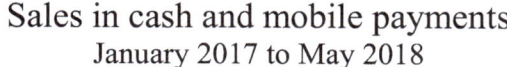

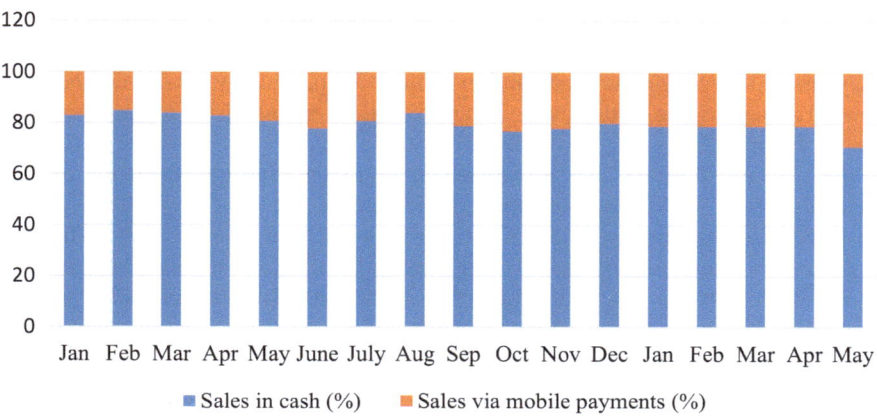

Fig. 7.2 Sales of Situation Stockholm in cash and via mobile payments 2017–2018. Source: Data provided by Situation Stockholm

The move toward cashless sales continued in 2015 when they started to use the new mobile payment service called Swish that was provided by the banks and had become a great success. At this time almost half of the adult Swedes had started to use Swish, and it had become a strong substitute to cash. This service proved to be simple to use, and the vendors as well as the buyers tended to prefer it over card payments. It also made it easier for Situation Stockholm to know how many magazines each vendor had sold and how much money they had generated. It became a win-win-win for vendors, buyers, and the organization. Later they also started to upgrade the Swish service in order to manage information and planning more efficiently.

This development has led to a situation where sales via mobile payment services—mainly Swish but also iZettle—are steadily over 20% of total sales and even reached 29% in May 2018 (Fig. 7.2).

The organization's demand on the payment services they use has also pushed suppliers to develop new features and improve their offers. They have, for instance, asked for administrative features enabling vendor-based reporting, location services based on GPS positioning, and QR code-based sales and information management. Situation Stockholm has become a demanding and innovation-oriented customer to the payment service providers.

In the spring of 2018, around 20–25% of sales of the magazine are via electronic payment services provided by iZettle and Swish, and the rest is via cash. The dominating payment service is notably still cash. You may of course argue that this proves the necessity of cash—and especially for the homeless people we are talking about. And you have a point. Some of the vendors and some buyers apparently prefer cash.

There is also another reason behind this. Even if almost everyone is entitled to a bank account in Sweden and Europe,[16] there are some exceptions, and the people selling Situation Stockholm falls in this category. Banks can refuse to provide a bank account to people who have problems identifying themselves, to people who cannot explain why they need an account and especially when there is a risk the account may be used for illegal purposes, and to people who previously have been dishonest toward a bank. Some of these aspects apply to the vendors of the magazine we are discussing here.

Most vendors do not have a bank account and are therefore restricted to using cash when they want to buy something, which means that some prefer being paid in cash but also that the operations must almost by default involve cash. When the organization Situation Stockholm—that receives the card and mobile payments into its bank account—is to pay vendors, they must use cash. Vendors often use the organization's account as a savings account and keep some of their money in this account—and thereby get indirectly banked!—but also receives some cash in order to buy the things they need to survive.

This indirect banking of the unbanked has—according to Jenny Lindroth—had the effect that the vendors have started to plan their private financial situation. They can save some money in the organization's account, receive some cash, and then invest some of their money in new magazines guaranteeing future income. In this way, they have become empowered to control their own life.

When I ask Jenny Lindroth in the spring of 2018 if they could stop accepting cash completely, she answers in a quick and straightforward way that they cannot! The organization cannot become entirely cashless since the vendors rely on cash. But Situation Stockholm has been and still is an influential driver of the transition of Stockholm toward a cashless city! And the adoption of noncash payment services helped the organization fulfill its objective to empower homeless people and make them having better control over their future by banking them.

And they helped teaching Stockholm how to use mobile payment services instead of cash.

The Swedish Church[17]: The Largest Church in Sweden

Sweden is a country where religion and parishes have had a central role in the society for a long time even if the average Swede generally say that he or she is not religious and is not attending parish ceremonies. Dagen,[18] which is a free magazine based on Christian beliefs, even claimed in 2009 that Sweden is one of the least religious countries in the world where only 17% of the population says that religion plays an

---

[16] https://www.swedishbankers.se/media/3688/1802_engelska.pdf

[17] Svenska Kyrkan https://www.svenskakyrkan.se/

[18] http://www.dagen.se/

important role in their lives.[19] A more recent study argues that Swedes relation to religion is complex and that the average Swede believes in some higher faith even if this belief often is not connected to one of the traditional religions.[20] Sweden can probably best be described as a highly secularized country where people believe in some form of higher beliefs.

The biggest parish in Sweden is called The Parish of Sweden and describes itself as a national parish that is open to everyone living in Sweden regardless of nationality.[21] It is an Evangelical Lutheran parish covering all of Sweden which is open to all, episcopal and democratic. It has 6.1 million members in a population of about 10 million Swedes which actually means that over 60% of Swedes belong to this parish.[22] Not bad in a secularized country! This parish is active in all parts of Sweden through its 3500 parishes in Sweden and 13 dioceses. It is financed via membership fees which are around 59% of total income and funeral fees around 19%, and the rest is financed mainly via offertories and other contributions as well as financial returns on assets. The activities of the parish is organized and operated via almost 3400 parishes and chapels in Sweden. One of these is Svenska Kyrkan in Sundbyberg which is located in the Stockholm area.

The Swedish Parish in Sundbyberg in Stockholm[23]: A Cash-Free Organization[24]

This parish has two parish buildings, one chapel, and its own funeral place which is not that common for parishes in the Stockholm area. It is more like a parish in the countryside than a parish in the city says the vicar Micke Åsman. The parish engages 40 persons including 6 vicars in addition to deacons, musicians, funeral service assistants, and other functions. It has a governing body called Kyrkofullmäktige which includes people that are elected in an open election every fourth year. This body, in turn, elects people that work in a board called Kyrkorådet which assumes the operative leadership of the parish. This body makes decisions on issues that concern the parish including budgets, employments, and other critical decisions. But it recently made a remarkably brave and modern decision. In 2018, Kyrkorådet in this parish decided to start operating their activities as a cashless parish, i.e., that offertories and other forms of payments to the parish no longer can be done in cash. Starting from February 1, 2018, the parish is cash-free. It only accepts gifts and

---

[19]http://www.dagen.se/sverige-ett-av-varldens-minst-religiosa-lander-1.175189

[20]https://www.forskning.se/2017/04/12/svenskarna-tror-men-inte-pa-gud/

[21]https://www.svenskakyrkan.se/

[22]www.svenskakyrkan.se/statistik

[23]https://www.svenskakyrkan.se/sundbyberg

[24]https://www.svenskakyrkan.se/sundbyberg

Fig. 7.3 The Swedish parish in Sundbyberg becomes cash-free. Source: https://www.
svenskakyrkan.se/sundbyberg/svenska-kyrkan-i-sundbyberg-blir-kontantfri

offertories via Swish or via direct debits. It is a test that is planned to continue
throughout 2018 (Fig. 7.3).

A Cash-Free Parish: Combining Sacred Traditions with Modern Technologies

The vicar Micke Åsman explains that one of the reasons behind the decision to stop
accepting cash is that this improves the working environment and safety of the
employees which is a central concern for the parish. The staff did not feel safe when
they had to go to the bank with a large amount of cash to deposit it. They feared
being robbed. It was also a cumbersome and time-consuming task to handle the cash
before it could be taken to the bank. In recent years the problem got even worse as
the local bank closed their cash handling services which meant they had to deposit
their cash in a grocery store in the neighboring municipality. On top of this, new
Swedish coins that came in 2015–2017 were even more difficult—at least in the
beginning before they had become used to them—to handle than the old coins. The
new bills and coins meant that more cash than usual came to the parish which
increased their problems. In the end, the problems had become too severe to handle.
    Another motivation behind the decision is that handling cash has become very
costly in relation to the relatively small amounts of cash that the parish is given each
year. The fees for cash-in-transit services are high, and banks' fees for depositing

cash are also high. Elisabeth Tunberg, Head of Administration, who has been working at a bank, says that she has asked banks to accept lower or even zero fees since the money is aimed for charity such as international aid related to humanitarian catastrophes, aid to people in need in Sweden and elsewhere, as well as aid to refugees. But the banks did not accept to drop fees. Over time the overall costs for handling cash had led to a situation where other activities of the parish were hurt because of the fees. This was not acceptable according to Micke Åsman.

It was also the case that the parish had no fees for concerts or other activities which meant that the decision to stop accepting cash did not lead to a situation where certain persons would become excluded or not feel welcome because they did not have access to cards or mobile payment services. The parish saw no distinct disadvantages by not accepting cash.

A third reason they mention is that the parish wants to adapt to the current society and its developments where cash is becoming used to a lesser and lesser extent.

> I am proud to say we are future oriented and contemporary. It is great to be able to combine the traditions of our parish with modern technologies of our society. We are probably the first parish in Sweden to do this and our colleagues around the country are curiously following what we are doing and want to hear about our experiences, says Micke Åsman.

He adds that cash often is used in the gray and black sectors of the society, and the parish therefore sees it as a positive thing to not encourage this. "We are contributing to a better society", says Micke.

The parish had started to accept mobile payments already in 2015 and felt they were experienced enough to be comfortable to stop accepting cash altogether. They were not anxious about the services or how to use them. And the final decision to stop accepting cash was unanimously taken by Kyrkorådet and the people working in the parish.

When the parish started to discuss the possibility of not accepting cash, there was an important discussion related to teleological beliefs. A fundamental belief in the parish is that one should share one's wealth with those in difficulties. Collecting gifts and offertories has therefore always been a central part of this. Some persons in the parish wondered if the decision to stop accepting cash actually goes against the theological conviction to donate to people in need. But it does not, according to Micke and Elisabeth. The parish is just changing the tools that are used to collect offertories, not the theological principles of offertories.

So has there not been complaints, I ask Micke Åsman and Elisabeth Tunberg. Has not your members complained, which is something you may expect since many of the most active parish members tend to be old and elderly tend to be the ones that are most in favor of cash? No, they say. There has only been one person that has complained—a 99-year-old woman who is really concerned about what happens if cash disappears. She argues that the democracy and free society will be hurt if cash disappears, which—one must add—is an opinion she shares with others[25] such as

---

[25] See, for instance, http://www.barometern.se/debatt/kontanter-en-demokratifraga/ as well as http://www.news55.se/artiklar/pro-och-spf-seniorerna-kontanthanteringen-ar-en-demokratifraga/

the organizations for elderly people in Sweden. But apart from this woman, the other members of the parish have adapted well.

So, what will happen after the test period is over, I ask. "I do not think we can reverse this decision", says Micke Åsman.

PRO: Pensioners Fighting to Keep Legal Tender in Sweden

PRO[26] or the Swedish National Pensioners' Organization is the largest organization for retired people in Sweden with around 350, 000 members organized in 1400 local units covering all of Sweden. PRO has three different pillars according to Ola Nilsson, PRO's expert in issues related to health and consumer politics, where the first one focuses on protecting the interests of their members and society at large. To achieve this, PRO is actively engaged in political debates on pension levels, taxes, social welfare, financial security, medical treatment, but also solidarity and discrimination in general. Here, access to cash has become an important question for PRO which is manifested in many initiatives. The second area concerns social meetings and shared activities among members, while the third one concerns education and training for members, which, for instance, involves training related to how to understand and manage the growth of digital services. One aim behind this particular course is to avoid or bridge digital divides in the Swedish society, which illustrates the challenge many elderly are facing in the digitalization of Sweden.

In April 2018 the British media agency BBC News described PRO's stance in the issue of cash with the words: "The Swedes rebelling against a cashless society."[27] It is without doubt that the pensioners in Sweden have become one of the strongest balancing forces against the quick development of a cashless society in Sweden (Fig. 7.4). The organization is not formally opposed to the concept of a cashless society, but they are worried about the speed through which this is happening and the lack of protection for the ones who suffer the most from a declining use of cash. They are also actively arguing that banks should take better responsibility and improve their cash handling services to customers.

In June 2016 PRO was engaged in a campaign called "Kontanter behövs"[28] where they argued cash must be kept in Sweden since there are groups in the society—elderly, people with disabilities, and people living in rural areas—that depend on cash and that the society therefore must work to protect cash. Their message was very much in line with the conclusions drawn in the annual reports on access to basic payment services made by the County Administrative Boards (Länsstyrelserna, 2017).

---

[26]Pensionärernas Riksorganisation www.pro.se

[27]http://www.pro.se/Gemenskap%2D%2Daktiviteter/Nyhetsarkiv/PRO-intervjuat-av-brittiska-BBC-angaende-kontantfragan/?id=270547&epslanguage=sv

[28]This is translated to "Cash is necessary" (author's translation).

The Swedes rebelling against a cashless society

By Maddy Savage
Business reporter, Stockholm

⊙ 6 April 2018   f 🐦 ◉ ✉ < Share

Fig. 7.4 PRO interviewed in BBC News. Source: BBC News https://www.bbc.com/news/busi ness-43645676

IN 2016, PRO managed to collect 139,064 signatures from people that supported their cause and handed these over to the Minister for Financial Markets and Consumer Affairs Per Bolund (Fig. 7.5).[29] The aim was to convince politicians that Sweden needed to take action to avoid problems as cash is disappearing but also to make sure cash does not disappear entirely.

"PRO welcomes digital payment solutions and educate our members to keep up with the development. Our congress in 2015 was even done digitally via note pads. But everyone need to keep up and no one can be left behind. That is the reason we

---

[29]http://www.government.se/government-of-sweden/ministry-of-finance/per-bolund/

Fig. 7.5 PRO handing over results from their campaign to Per Bolund in June 2016. Photo: Stefan Bladh

need cash in combination with other payment services," says the chairman of PRO Christina Tallberg in the PRO website.[30] In short, PRO argues that the Government of Sweden should review the mandate of the Riksbank so that it includes a more clearly stated responsibility that access to basic payment services, i.e., cash, must be available to all consumers and merchants in all parts of Sweden.[31]

A challenge for PRO related to cash is not only that their members often are dependent on cash and sometimes reluctant or perhaps not able to use digital payment services but also that PRO activities—like lotteries, meetings, and other events—use cash as a tool for payments from participants. Local PRO organizations then face problems when wanting to deposit cash into their bank accounts. This is costly, time-consuming, and risky if the overall sums are large. Such problems are not seen in the national PRO organization, however, since membership fees are paid via invoices and electronic transactions. The challenges are clearly greatest in the daily events and activities on the local level. And there is a lack of well-adapted digital services for these activities, says Ola Nilsson.

Ola Nilsson also provides examples of other problems like when banks set fees of 100 SEK for paper-based annual account reports—that are essential for each person's tax declarations—and fees of similar amounts if a person buys a ticket via

---

[30]This quote is translated from Swedish to English based on the text in the site http://pro.se/pension/ Nyhetsarkiv/139064-stodjer-PROs-kamp-for-kontanter/?id=184283&epslanguage=sv

[31]http://pro.se/Global/PRO%20riksorganisationen/Nyheter/Finansmarknadsminister.pdf

phone from railroad operators like SJ. It has become costly and inconvenient for people that—for one or another reason—prefer using cash instead of digital payment services. This does not, however, mean PRO is opposed to digitalization.

> The digitalization of our society is good and often makes things easier for our members but we must make sure the development is not too fast and that people are not forced to start using digital payment services when they are not able or willing to do this, says Ola Nilsson.

Another action of PRO was to lobby in relation to the current review of the central bank law[32] by arguing that the Riksbank's future responsibility in the payment system should protect the use of cash as long as it is legal tender and that there should be stricter requirements for commercial banks to offer cash handling services at the local level. PRO is proposing that at least one commercial bank should be required to offer these services in smaller cities. This is not just a question of having access to a service—it is more than that.

Having Access to Payment Services Is a Foundation for a Democracy

> Having access to basic payment services is a foundation of a democratic society, Each citizen has a democratic right to participate in the development of the society and not being able to make payments restricts a person's access to public and private services, and thus also the possibility to participate in the society, says Ola Nilsson.

He continues:

> Even if Sweden will become more and more digital, there will still be people who cannot or do not want to be fully digital and these persons must also be able to take part in the development of our society.

When I ask him about how he views the political debate on how cash is disappearing and which political actions that need to be taken, he states that he is not impressed. Politicians have answered well to some issues—like the need to change consumer protection related to sales via phone calls—but not that well related to the issue of access to cash. There are some politicians that are very active in this issue, but the majority is not. And, it does not seem to be possible to have a good political debate on this question. Access to cash was an important question in the political campaigns for the Swedish elections in 2018, concludes Ola. Not even PRO will focus on this issue. The overall level of pensions is prioritized.

---

[32]http://www.regeringen.se/rattsdokument/kommittedirektiv/2016/12/dir.-2016114/

The PRO Activities in Östersund Will Not Work Without Cash

"Our members need cash to make payments," says Elsy Sandbom who is working for PRO in Östersund, which is a city in the geographical center of Sweden. The city[33] has about 50,000 people and is the largest city in the Jämtland County. The area is most well-known for its outdoor winter sports profile including, for instance, skiing and mountaineering but recently also got a lot new attention as the city's football team beat Arsenal at Emirates Stadium, London, in the Europa League Cup.[34] The most important factor when we are to discuss cash, however, concerns the geographical distances and the dependence on cash.

There are smaller cities outside Östersund—like Gällö and Bräcke—where banks have closed down completely or only provide limited services which of course have made these areas difficult to live in for people that rely on cash. It is not unusual that the local grocery store is the only provider of cash services—both withdrawals and deposits—and thus in practice has replaced the banks in providing cash handling services. "The banks have a strange view on cash. They do not seem to understand our dependence on cash," says Elsy. In addition, many parts of their region may not have well-functioning and reliable Internet and telecommunication systems which make them also technologically dependent on cash.

Elderly often do not have access to computers, Internet, and smartphones and therefore become dependent on cash.

Our younger members that are around 70 may not have problems but our members in their 80s and 90s definitely have problems today. They want to use cash because they trust cash and are comfortable using cash. They feel naked without cash, says Elsy Sandbom.

The PRO organization also meet problems if they cannot use cash since the alternatives—like invoices or card payments—are expensive, time-consuming, and inconvenient according to Elsy. The organization organize coffee meetings, lotteries, bingo, and dances in which cash is a necessary service, and they do not know how they would be able to run these events if cash was not available.

When I was a kid we were keen to collect coins by doing small favors like opening gates to cars outside the church on Sundays. Then we could save these coins in a savings account that our school and local savings bank helped us start. But this was a long time ago. Banks are different now, says Elsy.

---

[33]http://www.ostersund.se/

[34]https://www.bbc.com/sport/football/43136849

Rural Sweden[35]: A GONGO

Rural Sweden is an organization that aims to make all parts of Sweden prosper and develop. It is a national civil society organization for rural development based on some 5000 local community groups and 40 member organizations representing all parts of Sweden. The organization is not large—the employed personnel equals eight FTE—but given they cooperate with all kinds of local organizations, the entire mass of the activities Rural Sweden initiates and supports become substantial and influential.

One of the reasons behind the need of this organization is the geographical structure of Sweden. Even if the country only has around 10.1 million people, it stretches an area of 447,435 km^2 which makes it the fifth largest country in Europe. And the population density by definition is very low with around 22.6 persons per km^2, which can be compared with around 411 persons per km^2 for the Netherlands and 368 persons per km^2 for Belgium. In short, there are on average large distances between Swedes which influence access to critical services like telephony, postal services, Internet access, and basic payment services.

As a result, rural areas tend to have much poorer access to these services than cities, which leads to the purpose and work of Rural Sweden:

> Our vision is to have vibrant local communities all over Sweden. We work towards balance between rural and urban areas, good rural development and just conditions and terms for the whole country.[36]

To achieve this, the organization has four prioritized areas including infrastructure and digitization, local services, culture, as well as local development. Access to basic payment services—like cash but also other services like schools, health care, policemen, and fire brigades—fall into these priorities. Four main values or ideals for their operations are democracy, diversity, sustainability, and equal opportunities.

> Our main challenges are to make sure local communities have access to public service, broadband, digitalized services, tools and methods to become empowered as well as having values and a local culture that stimulate young and old people to work for the development of the local community. This means we support many different initiatives in different local communities since regions tend to differ in their needs and challenges. We describe ourselves as a GONGO—a Governmental Non-Governmental Organization, says Ylva Lundkvist Fridh who is coordinating initiatives for local communities.

When discussing payment services, it becomes clear how the organization prioritizes ends over means. They work to make local communities develop and prosper, but they have a pragmatic approach to which payment services best help the community, its companies, and its people to prosper. The organization does not have a principle or basic conviction that cash must be kept.

---

[35]In Swedish: Hela Sverige ska leva https://www.helasverige.se/in-english/

[36]https://www.helasverige.se/in-english/

We actively support initiatives to make sure cash handling services are kept at the local levels—like the work done by the access to cash campaign—since people living in the local communities often prefer or even depend on cash. But our concern is that cash handling services are removed before new alternatives are developed, offered and accepted by the local communities. We see the same worrying trend that we saw when fixed landline telephone services were withdrawn before mobile network systems had been built in each local community that lost traditional telephone systems. We are afraid that we may see a new form of digital divide where some groups are left behind when new digital services are launched. But the communities we support are seldom obsessed with which payment service that is used as long as it works well, is reliable and liked by people and firms in the local community, says Ylva.

She continues: "We fight for the principle of equal right to public services in all parts of Sweden!" She also makes it clear that the organization as such do not use cash in their own operations; they prefer electronic bank transactions.

Another example is that Rural Sweden works with initiatives to improve the locally oriented financial system as they see how commercial banks tend to close their local offices. This includes not only access to basic payment services but also making sure there is access to funding and capital for small businesses aiming to provide products and services to the local community or even to expand their sales far beyond that.

It is clear that rural parts of Sweden face new challenges as cash disappears and that new innovative services are not yet a reliable substitute to cash in certain situations, for certain groups, and in certain geographical areas. The need of an organization like *Hela Sverige ska leva* is strong as Sweden is being transformed into a cash-free society.

The Story of These Stories

The stories show very different ways to survive and live in a society where cash is decreasing but where payments still need to be made and received. Some do not have any problems whatsoever, while others fight to adapt to a new situation. As we should expect with all major transformations of our societies, people adapt but some not without hard work and frustration. And few—if any—are unconcerned. Money matters!

If I am to summarize some of the main points in these stories, I would say that the issue of cash is an emotional one where viewpoints—even in the consensus-oriented Sweden—differ substantially. Many have strong emotions either in favor of or against cash, but the general consent is not that cash must be kept for its own sake. Many say it must be kept so that some groups—primarily elderly, people with disabilities, immigrants, and small businesses in rural areas—still can make and receive payments. The idea many state is that there must be usable, attractive alternatives in place before cash disappears completely.

There are also examples—like Situation Stockholm and donations in general—where the new innovative services help unbanked to become banked, at least in practical terms, as well as help to raise funding to people in need. We also saw a somewhat unexpected case where a parish in Stockholm has already decided to be cash-free during 2018.

There is—on the other hand—a movement aiming to keep cash or at least reduce the speed with which it disappears. They are working to make politicians aware of the problems and to start acting to handle the challenges that rise as cash disappears. The people in this movement often perform volunteer work to help local communities and people to handle the challenges they face. And we must not forget the work by the organizations for retired people and the lobbying from the Access to Cash Campaign.

All of these examples have aimed to provide a richer and deeper understanding of how people in Sweden think and act when it comes to cash in 2018.

References

Länsstyrelserna. (2017). *Bevakning av grundläggande betalningstjänster 2017*. Falun: Länsstyrelsen i Dalarna.

Perbo, U. (1999). Varför fick Sverige en depression i början av 90-talet. *Ekonomisk Debatt, 27*(6), 325–333.

Rogers, E. M. (2010). *Diffusion of innovations*. New York: Simon and Schuster.

Wiefels, P., & Moore, G. A. (2002). *The chasm companion: A fieldbook to crossing the chasm and inside the tornado*. New York: HarperBusiness.

Chapter 8
The Future of Cash in Sweden

Is a Cashless Economy Possible?

Many may argue that it is possible to see a society without cash. Cash is—as I have argued—one of the most important innovations in the history of humanity. Could and should we get rid of that? Many are convinced we must keep cash, while others welcome a transition toward a cashless society.

The US economist Kenneth S. Rogoff advocates a move toward a society with less cash in his book *The Curse of Cash* (Rogoff, 2016). The book concludes there are benefits from less cash since it discourages tax evasion and crime and enables governments and central banks to handle economic crises more effectively. One main reason being that the financial policies no longer would be limited by the "zero lower bound" interest rate, i.e., that the existence of cash makes it difficult to operate with negative interest rates since investors then can turn to cash instead of bonds with negative interest rates. Rogoff also states that illegal activities like organized crime, illegal immigration, and untaxed payments hurt the entire society and could be avoided—or at least made more difficult—if cash disappears. He also shows that this must be balanced against negative effects from less cash such as, for instance, the risk of financial exclusion of some groups if cash disappears.

Issuing cash has always been an instrument for a ruler—a king, queen, government, or dictator—to finance its own activities since the seignorage,[1] the difference between face value of cash and the production costs of cash, often is rather substantial. A question then is whether central banks risk to become financially dependent on governments if their ability to generate seignorage from cash disappears. This may in the end harm the ability for central banks to control the interest rate and to govern the domestic economic markets. Rogoff also acknowledges,

---

[1] Rogoff defines seignorage as "the difference between the face value of coints minted by the government and the cost of inputs, including both materials and production costs" (Rogoff, 2016, p. 81).

N. Arvidsson, *Building a Cashless Society*, SpringerBriefs in Economics,
https://doi.org/10.1007/978-3-030-10689-8_8

however, that seignorage in Sweden actually already is negative[2] which implies that this risk does not seem to be critical for the independence of the Riksbank. And it is of course also possible to gain seignorage if a central bank issues digital currencies, i.e., CBDC, which the Riksbank is considering to do.[3] A central bank may also fund itself via margins between lending and borrowing. Having central banks that do not issue cash is a possibility (Segendorf & Wilbe, 2014). The central bank of law of Sweden is currently being reviewed where one question concerns the role of cash in Sweden.[4]

Rogoff (2016, Chap. 7) actually outlines a top-down-driven plan for how central banks and governments can address the move toward a cash-free society. This is built on first phasing out large value bills until only small bills or even coins remain. The next step is to develop policies ensuring financial inclusion for all. A situation with a digital divide and financial exclusion is simply not acceptable. The third step is to enforce regulation and laws ensuring privacy and integrity for people making electronic payments. Money and payments are built on trust, and if people are worried about privacy and integrity when making payments, they will not these services. The last step is to build infrastructure—clearing and settlement systems—that enables real-time payments or close to real-time payments. This will make the electronic payment services provide the same value proposition as cash, i.e., the ability to transfer value in a second or two. Just like what happens when we make a cash payment, but electronically. Rogoff acknowledges this is a slow, gradual process without a clear aim to get rid of cash entirely. The slowness enables the system to handle challenges that are not foreseen.

If the Riksbank of Sweden had seen Rogoff's plan, the parliament[5] or the Riksbank should of course have gotten rid of the largest Swedish bill—the 1000 SEK bill—when introduced new cash. But they did not. This confirms that it is not politicians and the Riksbank that drives the process toward less cash in Sweden. But the central bank does not seem to be strongly opposed it either since it acknowledges that a central bank could stop issuing cash and is also looking at the alternative of providing electronic central bank money.

Several central banks around the world are considering the possibility to launch central bank digital currencies, i.e., digital cash backed by the central bank and the

---

[2]Sweden actually had a negative seignorage during the period 2006–2015 (Rogoff, 2016, p. 84) which is related to the decreased use of cash in Sweden and in particular the decrease of the nominal value of cash in circulation.

[3]http://www.riksbank.se/Documents/Avdelningar/AFS/2017/Projektplan%20e-kronan_170314_eng.pdf

[4]http://www.regeringen.se/rattsdokument/kommittedirektiv/2016/12/dir.-2016114/

[5]http://www.riksbank.se/Documents/Protokollsbilagor/Fullmaktige/2014/probil_fullm_bilaga_B2_140822.pdf

government.[6] The Bank of England,[7, 8] the Bank of Canada,[9] and the Riksbank[10, 11] are just some examples (see also discussion in Arvidsson, 2018). The Riksbank in Sweden has outlined different areas in which they need to make decisions if they are to introduce digital cash that is backed by the central bank. These areas concerns which technologies to use, which devices that may be used, which policies to develop, and which legal requirements that must be addressed. The Riksbank is clearly formulating this as a possibility that needs to be studied, and the decision to actually realize this or not will be taken in the end of 2018.

The Committee of Inquiry on the Riksbank is currently reviewing how the Riksbank's responsibility for effective cash management throughout Sweden should be clarified in law.[12] Given the reduced access to cash in the Swedish society and the problems this creates for some groups, the Swedish parliament decided to start a thorough inquiry of whether the central bank law and demands on commercial banks must be changed in order to ensure an efficient and secure system for cash payments in Sweden. The interim report is proposing actions and requirements in a new system for cash handling which would, if realized, increase the demand on commercial banks to deliver cash handling services in all parts of Sweden.[13]

The report states:

> In the Committee's view, access to cash withdrawals and the possibility for businesses and associations to deposit their daily receipts must be improved to strengthen cash's position in society. Initiatives should primarily target rural areas, where access to cash services is already significantly more limited with respect to distance than in the rest of the country and where there is greatest risk that cash-in-transit and cash services will disappear completely (SOU, 2018:42, page 24)

The interim report proposes that essentially all Swedes—99 out of 100—and businesses should have access to cash withdrawal services as well as cash deposit services within 25 km from where they live and/or operate their businesses. And it is the largest banks—the ones offering consumer payment accounts and having more than 70 billion SEK in deposits—that should supply these services. These banks are regarded to be critical for the cash system and have national coverage of services, which today means that five banks and one foreign credit institution—SEB, Svenska

---

[6]There are studies indicating positive macroeconomic gains if a central bank introduces a "central bank digital currency" (CBDC) as, for instance, Barrdear and Kumhof (2016).

[7]http://www.bankofengland.co.uk/research/Pages/onebank/cbdc.aspx

[8]For a full list of research questions, see http://www.bankofengland.co.uk/research/Documents/onebank/cbdc.pdf

[9]http://www.bankofcanada.ca/

[10]http://www.riksbank.se/sv/Press-och-publicerat/Riksbanken-Play/Skingsley-Borde-Riksbanken-ge-ut-e-kronor

[11]http://www.riksbank.se/Documents/Avdelningar/AFS/2017/Projektplan%20e-kronan_170314_eng.pdf

[12]https://www.regeringen.se/rattsliga-dokument/kommittedirektiv/2016/12/dir.-2016114/

[13]https://www.regeringen.se/rattsliga-dokument/statens-offentliga-utredningar/2018/06/sou-201842/

Handelsbanken, Nordea Bank, Swedbank, Länsförsäkringar Bank, and Danske Bank—would need to follow these requirements.

The report argues that costs related to supplying these services are not extensive and suggest there will be some sort of fines or sanctions if banks fail to meet these requirements. Moreover, it states that the role of the Riksbank in the cash handling system must be clarified in law especially related to monitoring and analyzing cash handling as well as to report this to the Swedish parliament. The interim report is currently under review.

The Swedish Bankers' Association is critical to the propositions in the interim report. The bankers argues that there is no motivation behind the propositions, that there are arguments speaking against the conclusions, and that it is not correct to name a few banks and institutions that should provide these services.[14] They also argue that these recommendations may contradict other laws, that they do not ensure actual services will be provided at the places where they are needed, and that sanctions are disproportionate. Not surprisingly, banks are negative toward the interim report propositions. It is not very brave to conclude the report will lead to an engaged debate about the future of cash in Sweden and the legal framework around cash.

When discussing possible changes in the roles of commercial banks and the Riksbank, we must of course also dig deeper into the Riksbank's e-krona project. The Riksbank is studying the possibility to launch an e-krona, which can be described as digital cash issued by the central bank of Sweden or more formally as a central bank digital currency (CBDC). The Riksbank has not yet decided whether they will launch an e-krona or not but is pursuing the project as a possible action to meet the rapid decline of cash in Sweden.[15]

The Riksbank states:

An e-krona would give the general public access to a digital complement to cash, for which the state would guarantee the value of the money, a form of digital central bank money. At present, the Riksbank only offers banks and other RIX participants digital money, the other digital money in society is private bank money issued by commercial banks.[16]

Their project started in 2017 and has studied different options they may choose between, which properties this possibility should have, the legal implications around the idea, and also reviewed proposals for possible technologies. The motivation is that a society and an economic system are stabilized and made more efficient if there is central bank money that is at the core of the system. This form of money is more stable and reliable since it is issued by a central bank through the mandate given by a government and thereby represents a direct claim on the Swedish state, whereas bank money—the money in our bank accounts—is a claim on the bank we have as our bank. In the end, the reliability and strength of the money we have are decided by the actor toward whom our claims are made. If we have cash or possible e-kronor

---

[14]https://www.swedishbankers.se/media/3916/f181015y.pdf

[15]https://www.riksbank.se/en-gb/payments%2D%2Dcash/e-krona/

[16]https://www.riksbank.se/en-gb/payments%2D%2Dcash/e-krona/

denominated in SEK, we have a claim on the state of Sweden. If we have money deposited in a bank account, we have a claim on that bank. So, who do you trust the most?

We cannot be 100% certain the state will redeem our claims and maintain a stable currency—as we have seen throughout history—but I would definitely argue that a claim on the state of Sweden is better than a claim on a commercial bank. And most will agree. So there is a role to play for central bank money also in a cash-free society. An e-krona may play the same role as cash used to do, and the Riksbank is continuing their work to develop this.[17]

We should at the same time acknowledge that regulation and legislation governing banks are aimed at guaranteeing that consumers and businesses do not lose their deposits—claims—on a commercial bank if it ends up in a situation where its assets do not cover their debts, i.e., face bankruptcy. The central bank and the government may act as lender of last resort in order to make sure people and businesses do not lose their assets, there are deposit guarantee legislations covering up to 100,000 Euro for deposits made in banks, and there are regulations overseeing banks in order to avoid bankruptcies.

Swedish banks are not positive vis-à-vis an e-krona since they argue it will not play an important role in the Swedish payment system and that it even will make the Riksbank with an e-krona a potential competitor to savings or transaction accounts provided by commercial banks, which is something the Riksbank by law cannot do. The Riksbank is not allowed to compete with commercial banks, and an e-krona that is deposited in an account provided by the state—for instance, in a tax account managed by the tax authorities—may become a competitive service compared to transaction accounts provided by commercial banks. The Swedish Bankers' Association has even warned the Riksbank to issue an e-krona.[18]

Once again we see that money provided by a central bank—in the form of cash or possibly digital forms—creates discussions and heated debates. Money matters!

Today we are intrigued and fascinated by new forms of money and payments that seem to pop out of entrepreneurs' minds almost every day. There are more than 2000 different types of cryptocurrencies.[19] The main cryptocurrencies include Bitcoin, Ethereum, XRP, Bitcoin Cash, EOS, Stellar, and Litecoin. It is without doubt these alternative forms of currencies have made a strong impact on the banking and payment industry where the current value of Bitcoins is around 112 billion USD, the value of Ethereum is around 21 billion USD, the current value of XRP is around 18 billion USD, and the current value of Bitcoin Cash is close to 8 billion USD.[20]

---

[17]https://www.riksbank.se/en-gb/payments%2D%2Dcash/e-krona/e-krona-reports/e-krona-pro ject-report-2/

[18]https://www.affarsvarlden.se/bors-ekonominyheter/bankforeningen-varnar-riksbanken-for-e-kronan-6910428

[19]https://coinmarketcap.com/all/views/all/

[20]https://coinmarketcap.com/all/views/all/

Cryptocurrencies may at the moment together be valued to around 209 billion USD. This is impressive.

But we also see rather high volatility in the exchange rates of these currencies which means they are not meeting one critical demand, i.e., store of value that we put on efficient payment methods. The future of cryptocurrencies is very interesting, and these new forms of money and their underlying technology—block chains and distributed ledgers—are expected to revolutionize banking in general and payments in particular. In addition to the many other industries that will be disrupted via these technologies.

A possibility is that if central banks start to issue digital currencies, i.e., CBDCs, they will use the block chain technology to build and operate these currencies and the transactions connected to them. Even if I do not expand my discussion of these new technologies, it is without doubt they have an important role to play in the future payment system. We do not yet know which role they will play, but they will definitely play an important role.

New technologies also open up opportunities for new actors to enter the industry based on innovative services, and if this at the same time is stimulated by changed regulations, we can expect drastic transformations of both services and service providers. An important regulation that is changing the payment landscape at the moment is the second Payment Service Directive (PSD2) from the European Union. Some of its main aims are to increase competition and to stimulate innovation in the field of payments by institutionalizing an industry characterized by open banking.

Open banking is based on the simple idea that a bank account—usually the account where employees receive their wages and salaries—constitutes the centerpiece upon which other financial and payment services are built. When discussing payment services, we see that all services—cash, cards, mobile payment services, or other forms—build on the connection to a central account from which money is drawn when a payment is made. Since these centerpiece accounts—almost by definition—have been provided by commercial banks, these banks have had a natural opportunity to provide payment services connected to the account in question This firsthand access to customers' account enables banks to sell additional services relatively easy, and they often supply a package of services connected to the centerpiece account. As customers also tend to be loyal to their main bank, these banks have had a privileged position for many years. But the intention of open banking is to change this.

A key feature of PSD2 and open banking is that new forms of payment service providers—like payment initiation service providers (PISPs) or account information service providers (AISPs)—should be able to build their services directly connected to a person's bank account if that person allows them to do this. As the software governing bank accounts also should build on open application programming interfaces (APIs), a PISP or an AISP can build their services connected to the account without being hindered by the bank and its software specificities.

We can compare open APIs with electric sockets. What? Well, I mean that electric sockets have been standardized so that everyone knows exactly the characteristics of the electricity in the system as well as the physical appearance of the sockets. Even if this—for some unclear reason—still differs between countries, we can be certain of the standard within a country. This also means that any product that relies on electricity can use the electricity if they only adapt the standard setting. Toothbrushes, computers, ovens, refrigerators, dishwashers, lamps, and so on can use the same electricity. By setting this standard, any type of product can use the same electricity. So, by setting a standard—open APIs—for the systems handling accounts, any type of service can connect to a bank account and realize its value.

In essence, this means that banks all of a sudden is facing potential competition in a new way. They have been used to compete with other banks, but now they are facing competition from start-up, Fintech companies that are created in a new era based on new ideas and new systems. This requires new skills and roles from the traditional banks.

At the same time, we see a new generation—the millennials[21]—entering the banking markets who seem to have new demands and less loyalty to traditional banks than the previous consumer generations. They are also seem to have different forms of needs and demands and are perhaps more attracted by start-ups than by the old, retail banks. This is, at least, what many believe is about to happen.

All these events and changes point to an interesting future, and I conclude there is no law of nature stating that a central bank always will issue cash as legal tender.

The Future of Cash in Sweden

I have already concluded that Sweden is internationally unique in its low and rapidly decreasing use of cash. As of today there are few signs that this development will not continue. The speed of the decrease in the use of cash and instead favor electronic payment services will most likely fall, but the trend is likely to continue in the coming years.

Whenever you are saying something about the future, you need to open to the likelihood that you not be entirely correct. There are always events that cannot be foreseen and that may change the future in ways we cannot imagine. This does not mean I will refrain from discussing the future though. There are techniques—like scenario analysis—that are helpful tools to learn how to prepare for the future (Ramirez & Wilkinson, 2016). There are always some trends in a society that are highly likely to remain for some time and that therefore can be used as a foundation even for the future.

It is of course also possible to collect data about the future or rather data on what different actors believe about the future. So we did just that. We ran a large survey with Swedish merchants in 2017 where we asked them if they accept cash, if they are

---

[21]https://www.forbes.com/sites/shamahyder/2015/02/25/millennials-and-money-how-banks-are-missing-the-mark/#4f66363769b5

considering to stop accepting cash, which costs they face for different payment services, and a lot of other questions (Arvidsson, Hedman, & Segendorf, 2018).

Given the answers from 741 merchants in Sweden who rather well represent all the merchants in the most cash-intensive merchant industries, we were able to understand how the immediate future may look like. Today 97% of the merchants accept cash, but many are thinking about stopping to accept cash. In fact, if the beliefs from merchants turn out to become true, Sweden may become a practically cashless society in 2023. Our projection indicates that the average merchant in Sweden will not make a profit from cash-based sales in 2023 if the current development continues.

We conclude that merchants do not seem to be worried by costs behind accepting cash. Tangible costs for this are fees to service companies and equipment for cash handling, and these are often well-known by merchants. Less tangible costs like man-hours needed to handle cash and costs related to the risk of being robbed seem to be less well-known, however. All in all this makes merchants to underestimate actual costs for cash-based sales. Our study found that merchants in general seem to believe that their costs for cash-based sales are acceptable, while their costs for card-based sales are too high even though their actual costs for accepting cards are significantly lower than their actual costs for accepting cash.

I can list a number of factors making me conclude the reduction of cash will continue but of course some factors speaking in the other direction, i.e., that cash will not disappear but instead remain as an important way to make a payment in Sweden (Table 8.1). When looking at the entire list of factors influencing the future use of cash in Sweden, I draw the conclusion that there are more factors leading to less use of cash than there are factors preserving cash, which is a clear indication the process will perhaps be halted but not stopped. A critical counterforce, i.e., preserving cash, is of course a changed law forcing banks to provide cash handling services and thereby making a case for continued use of cash.

Table 8.1 Factors leading toward a cash-free society and factors preserving cash

Factors leading toward a cash-free society	Factors preserving cash
• Laws allowing cashless stores • Salaries paid into bank accounts • System for card payments • Laws on bank secrecy yielding trust in electronic services • Outsourced cash system making it demand-driven combined with curious and skilled consumers • Unions lobbying against cash for safety reasons • Laws forcing retailers to report sales to tax authorities • Tax incentives making household services "white" • Business models meaning cash is not profitable for banks • Crimes leading retailers to not accept cash • Innovative services substitute cash • Youngsters use electronic solutions • Fintech and IT firms create innovative payment services • Co-opetition realize interoperable, digital platforms but also energize creativity and efficiency • Importance of central bank money trigger ambition to create central digital currencies	• Problems for elderly, disabled, immigrants, and small firms leading to political action • Lobbying from interest groups (Access to Cash Campaign and interest group for elderly) to keep cash • A political aim to avoiding a "single point of failure" structure in the payment system[a] in combination with other work aiming to safeguard against cyber threats in the payment system[b] • Importance of reliability in retail payment systems • Importance of central bank money in the economy which trigger a political interest to keep cash • New legislation aiming to make sure cash handling is provided in all parts of Sweden

Source: Author's own illustration
[a]See, for instance, Engert, Fung, and Hendry (2018)
[b]https://www.riksdagen.se/sv/dokument-lagar/dokument/interpellation/kontanthantering-under-kris_H510351

References

Arvidsson, N. (2018). Chapter 4: The future of cash. In R. Teigland, S. Siri, A. Larsson, A. M. Puertas, & C. I. Bogusz (Eds.), *The rise and development of FinTech–Accounts of disruption from Sweden and beyond* (Routledge International Studies in Money and Banking) (pp. 85–98). London: Routledge.

Arvidsson, N., Hedman, J., & Segendorf, B. (2018). *När slutar svenska handlare acceptera kontanter?* (Handelsrådet, Forskningsrapport 2018:1).

Barrdear, J., & Kumhof, M. (2016). *The macroeconomics of central bank issued digital currencies.*

Engert, W., Fung, B. S. C., & Hendry, S. (2018). *Is a cashless society problematic?* (Staff Discussion Paper 2018-12). Bank of Canada.

Ramirez, R., & Wilkinson, A. (2016). *Strategic reframing – The Oxford scenario planning approach.* Oxford: Oxford University Press.

Rogoff, K. S. (2016). *The curse of cash.* Princeton, NJ: Princeton University Press.

Segendorf, B., & Wilbe, A. (2014). *Economic commentaries.*

SOU. (2018:42). *Tryggad tillgång till kontanter – delbetänkande av Riksbankskommitten.*

Chapter 9
What Can Be Learnt
from This Development?

One important lesson from this story of how Sweden is becoming a cashless society is that the process—if becoming cashless is seen as a goal—cannot be governed from above. A top-down driven approach is not likely to succeed as a stand-alone strategy. This is not to say that governments and central banks should leave it to the market.

No, I am saying that the most critical challenge is to stimulate bottom-up incentives and a will to replace cash with electronic services. Remember that money is nothing but trust in that the service I am using will allow me to use the value I expect to have in a transaction sometime in the future. History tells us that this trust cannot be commanded from the top; it can only be upheld—and potentially destroyed—from the top. Trust comes from below.

To rephrase myself: the time when rulers—kings and governments—could design the monetary system almost entirely by themselves is over. There are still strong reasons that governments and central banks should keep the power and control over money, but they need to realize that one effect from Internet is that their power is reduced. Internet functions as a new form of check to balance the power of governments and financial institutions.

Satoshi Nakamoto writes in the first sentence that one motivation behind a peer-to-peer network like Bitcoin is to launch:

> A purely peer-to-peer version of electronic cash would allow online payments to be sent directly from one party to another without going through a financial institution (Nakamoto, 2008, p. 1)

This new challenge—a potential substitute to the traditional money from nation states or simply a healthy competitor—means that central banks need to motivate their money by providing a secure, efficient, and trustworthy system. And, trust comes from below.

Creating this trust can be a challenge, though. First and foremost people need to trust the political and legal system, which seems to be a rising challenge for many nations today. They must trust they live in a good society! Then they need to trust the

N. Arvidsson, *Building a Cashless Society*, SpringerBriefs in Economics, https://doi.org/10.1007/978-3-030-10689-8_9

banking and financial system and the organizations providing services in general and their specific service provider in particular. Consumers' trust in electronic systems is yet another form of trust that is essential. In the end they must also trust the ones they transact with, i.e., they must trust they get whatever they purchase via the service they use. There are many layers of trust where each is important. As you know, the chain is not stronger than its weakest link, and so on.

But just to be clear, there is no central plan by the Swedish government and/or the central bank to get rid of cash. It should be noted though that neither of them seem to be negative to this development and that some decisions, like the privatization of cash handling and introduction of new bills and coins, may have stimulated the move toward less cash.

If there is to be a top-down plan to reduce the use of cash in a society, it can of course involve certain items. As discussed by Rogoff (2016) and others, reducing or deleting the high-value denominated bills is an obvious and rather easy measure to realize. This will of course need decisions from governments and central banks which may be a tricky challenge, for instance, in a complicated political arena as the European Union but relatively easy for single nation governments striving to reduce the use of cash.

Given there is a well-functioning infrastructure and services as well as a good uptake of those services, this measure should not be too problematic. It necessitates a high use of electronic accounts, wage and salaries being paid to electronic accounts, and high diffusion of services like cards, mobile payment services, invoicing or e-invoicing, direct debit solutions, and Internet banking. If this is in place, the challenge should not be that high.

Another critical thing is time. It does not only take two to tango—it also takes time to learn how to tango! The transformation in Sweden started—as shown in this book—several decades ago and has been developing since, sometimes very slowly and sometimes quite rapidly. But if some of the critical factors are not in place, the process is likely to become halted. This means that patience is important. Some critical aspects such as making sure that people have electronic accounts, that payment services are not too expensive, that companies pay salaries and wages into electronic accounts, that merchants must have cash register machines that cannot be manipulated, that tax authorities oversee cash-intensive industries, and that the ones most in need of cash can find strong, electronic alternatives need to be done. The question is if governments are willing to do it.

Then there are other challenges that need time. The majority of elderly that have been born and raised in a cash-based society are not likely to start using smartphones, apps, and advanced payment services. Some of these will gladly start using the new solutions or even traditional solutions as cards, but there will be a large group that will not. They will nevertheless have to be able to receive and make payments. And they are likely to live quite long as the average life expectancy seems to be increasing by the hour. There must be solutions also for this group.

To keep on providing central bank cash is one alternative, but what if those selling services will stop accepting it (as they can in Sweden)? Laws saying that cash must be provided by banks and accepted by merchants are a solution. Another alternative would be to stimulate innovation of electronic services aiming particularly for this group. Given that this group—the ones borne in the 1930s, 1940s, and 1950s—also is quite wealthy, it would actually be strategically unwise for service providers *not* to launch services for the group.

Do not tell this to others, but I can recommend you to take a serious look into the strategic value of developing payment services for the groups that are the least willing to use them. Not only is there valuable learning to be done, your image may in fact receive a golden blast.

Other groups that service providers should study and develop services for—and that also seem to be growing in our societies—are those with physical and cognitive disabilities. In research on innovation, it is often said that a company should work with the demanding customers in order to develop the most powerful innovations since this increases the likelihood that the innovations will succeed and be sustainable over time.

People with disabilities should therefore—if you ask me—be seen a group not only in need of valuable payment services when cash disappears but also a group that providers should see as highly demanding users that will force the companies to provide highly advanced and competitive solutions. The problem for companies is that they have read too much about innovation diffusion (Rogers, 2010) and chasms (Wiefels & Moore, 2002) and therefore tend to only focus on the user groups that have been called innovators and early adopters (Rogers, 2010).

Why not focus on the needs of the late majority and perhaps even laggards in Sweden to build services that later can be exported to other markets? Given the profitability in the payment industries, it seems to be a poor decision to not invest at least some of the overall investment budgets to develop solutions for the most cash needy consumer groups. And then governments and their financially as well as innovation oriented authorities could step in to stimulate such innovation.

It is not an easy task for public authorities to stimulate innovation though. The Swedish Post and Telecom Authority (PTS)[1] and the County Administrative Boards in Sweden[2] jointly have the responsibility to supervise and ensure that merchants and people have access to basic payment services. Given the observations that access to cash is decreasing in Sweden, they launched a public procurement of innovative payment services in 2016 with a focus on the groups facing problems as cash services disappear.

I was engaged as an expert in this public procurement, and this challenging but highly interesting task proved difficult. The final report of this initiative[3] showed that few tenders had been given and that the procurement process had to be closed without giving anyone the assignment to realize an innovative service. Reasons behind the lack of proposals included firms' uncertainty about innovation

---

[1]www.pts.se

[2]http://www.lansstyrelsen.se

[3]http://www.lansstyrelsen.se/Dalarna/Sv/publikationer/rapporter-2017/Pages/innovation-betal-2017.aspx?keyword=innovationsupphandling

procurement processes including the potential upsides as well as the risks, questions related to aspects of possible cooperation with competitors to build digital platforms, and the potential profits and sales from the service in question.

The perhaps most positive result from the procurement initiative was an improved dialogue between the authorities and the market actors on these societal challenges. Another result was the insight that the technologies and services to ensure access to basic payment services for the groups in questions already exists. It is more a matter of providers' attention to and interest in servicing these groups. All in all, the procurement initiative was needed and positive in the sense that it initiated a mutual learning process around innovation to replace cash even if it ended in a disappointment that a solution could not be procured.

In addition to performing innovation procurement of payment services that may replace cash for the ones most dependent upon cash, governments and other organizations are advised to educate citizens on risks and possibilities connected to electronic payments if compared to cash as well as on how to behave in a digital world. There is a need for popular education, i.e., free and voluntary education, on how to survive, live, and prosper in a digital society. Younger people and those highly interested in digital solutions may not be in need of such education and training, but others are.

As Sweden was transformed into an industrial society in the 1800s and early 1900s, there grew a need for people to understand how to handle money as they all of a sudden were paid by the hour, faced risks of becoming unemployed, and developed new habits that led to new expenses. In 1926, the savings banks started a magazine for children called *Spara och slösa* (save and waste) where one could follow the lives of two young girls called Spara and Slösa. One was very careful with money and made sure she always saved whatever she did not spend on critical things like food and clothes, while the other wasted her money on just about everything. The pedagogical message was clear: one should save one's well-earned money.

This was of course a nice way to sell banking services but also a way to educate people to live in an increasingly monetized society. I believe we need new forms of popular education training people—old and young—how to manage their private finances in a digital society. All with an aim to avoid a digital divide where some groups in the society are left behind in the digital era. We do *not* want a digital divide between digital natives and analog hermits!

Money is about trust, and it is likely that a smaller country with high trust in politicians and the banking system, like Sweden, is more likely to decrease the use of cash if compared to a larger country or economic zone where these are larger geographic and cultural distance between citizens and politicians. The smallness of our country is therefore a reason why there is so little cash, but this may also serve as a safeguard against the risk of a digital divide.

The country's tradition of social welfare and concern for all will hopefully serve as a force to make the transition toward a cashless society positive in the sense that it will not create a group of people that live outside the system and that is hurt by this transformation. Trust is likely to disappear if politicians, authorities, and/or banks do not acknowledge and work to solve these challenges. Such a mistake is actually something to highlight in a list of factors that may alter the development and turn Sweden into a country where cash is still king (or at least used and hailed).

Yet another aspect relates to work environments in the organizations accepting payment services. It is definitely advisable for employees and unions as well as employers and managers to build an opinion around the relationship between work safety and payment services. We all know that money as well as merchandise attracts criminals and that merchants and stores are potential victims of robberies. No matter whether such crimes are violent or not, it is critical to understand how to avoid such crimes and what to do if they occur.

One reason that Sweden is using little cash was that the unions started to act and lobby to reduce the use of cash in order to reduce the risk of robberies and that employees faced physical or psychological harm. No matter whether a store is vulnerable in the sense that cash or electronic money may become stolen, employers and employees must understand how to best protect this value as well as employees. This is a priority that should be acknowledged and be weighed in when making decisions about which payment services to accept and how to protect against theft and robberies. The conclusion by unions in Sweden in this matter—in banking, retail, and public transportation—was to lobby for a reduction of cash in stores.

One could of course also argue that new forms of payment services will stimulate new forms of crimes and that a reduction of cash will not mean a reduction of crimes. This is true and puts the finger on a critical challenge: any person and any business must be able to safeguard their money and their health no matter which money and payment services we use. Another critical part in the move toward a cash-free society is evidently to learn how to limit and handle crimes.

An eternal challenge related to the development of new digital payment services concerns the balance between cooperation and competition. As discussed previously, a payment service that is to be valuable to payer and payees but at the same time provide value to the providers necessitates large numbers of users on both sides of a payment. The ideal is many payers and many payees connected to the same digital platform. But the flip side to this is of course the risk of too dominating players that builds oligopolistic or even monopolistic profitability.

Having open platforms where providers supply competitive services from which payees and payers can select services based on their own preferences could be a solution to this challenge. This is what the open banking concept aims to do. But then there will of course be the question of who will provide the open platform since this actor will have a strong position in the entire value-creating system.

This means that antitrust authorities, central banks, and financial supervisory agencies need to combine forces—or at least share views—on how to balance the tricky paradox of competition versus collaboration for the creation of digital platforms for payment services and especially those aiming to help the most cash-dependent actors in the society since this is a group which banks and Fintech companies seemingly tend to forget.

There are several factors enabling and constituting a cash-free society, but the main challenge is to create trust in an efficient and reliable payment service for many—or even all—people (Table 9.1).

Table 9.1 Factors in the foundation of a digital payment system

• Making sure wages and salaries are paid directly into electronic accounts
• Stimulate citizens to have electronic accounts—avoid un-banked people
• Stimulating electronic payment services with the same functionality as cash, i.e., real-time clearing and settlement and confirmation to both payer and payee
• Strong laws and regulation to protect privacy as well as to protect people's money
• General trust by citizens into the payment system and its actors and especially the bank or banks whose services they are using
• Handling the balance between ensuring the existence of central bank money issued by the state and the central bank while at the same time realizing a business environment characterized by a level playing field where valuable innovation is possible
• General trust by citizens into the democratic system including the government and its politicians, legal framework including the court system and the police, monetary policies, critical institutions like central banks and financial supervisory agents, media, and others
• Trust by merchants into providers of payment and other services related to payments
• To decide whether cash is legal tender for all in all situations so that merchants cannot say no to cash or if this can be decided via negotiations between payers and payees
• Trust by citizen into merchants and others selling goods and services
• A general interest among consumers to be critical and curious buyers and users of payment and other services
• Designing the tax system and its actions to harmonize with innovations in the field of payments to ensure positive benefits from renewal can be realized, and negative effects from tax evasion can be avoided
• Collaboration between concerned authorities to realize co-opetition, i.e., to stimulate competition while at the same time ensure the growth of digital platforms that realize economies of scale and scope as well as interoperability and open access. One particularly important aspect related to competition and innovation is to stimulate start-up creations in the Fintech and Regtech industries perhaps related to technologies such as block chains
• Acknowledging a wide array of aspects such as avoiding a digital divide where some groups in our societies are marginalized due to lack of access to basic payment services, ensuring safety and protection for companies and people whose access to money may trigger robberies and theft, as well as long-term positive economic effects and export opportunities from companies being in the forefront of developing new technologies and services

Source: Author's own illustration

References

Nakamoto, S. (2008). *Bitcoin: A peer-to-peer electronic cash system.*

Rogers, E. M. (2010). *Diffusion of innovations.* New York: Simon and Schuster.

Rogoff, K. S. (2016). *The curse of cash.* Princeton, NJ: Princeton University Press.

Wiefels, P., & Moore, G. A. (2002). *The chasm companion: A fieldbook to crossing the chasm and inside the tornado.* New York: HarperBusiness.

Chapter 10
Summary and Conclusions

The development in Sweden has a long tradition from the middle of the twentieth century where actions and cooperation between critical actors have promoted electronic payment services. This has created a banking and payment system where the backbone is made of electronic bank accounts into which wages and salaries are paid which then serves as the base for all kinds of payments. The payment system is constituted on these accounts and payment services—cash, cards, invoices, Internet banking, mobile payments, and others—must connect to them. The inner "DNA" of the system is electronic.

Today we see a strong substitution effect where mobile payment services—like Swish and iZettle—replace cash payments, which means that the use of cash is decreasing rapidly. The value of cash in circulation in Swedish crowns dropped 50% between the peak in 2007 and the low figures of 2018. This has led Sweden to become the country in the world with the lowest use of cash.[1]

There are of course many reasons behind this development, and this book has pointed at many. One important reason is that politicians during the last 20 years have left the development of payment services to the market, i.e., it is banks, card operators, payment receivers, payment service providers, telecom operators, automated clearing houses, payers, etc. that determine the development of the system. In the end it is the demand from consumers that set the limits to the use of cash, and they are seemingly more interested in using electronic services than cash. The laws and the system governing cash handling stimulate a reduction of cash.

If we turn our eyes to the future, me and my colleagues argue that Sweden may become a practically cashless society, but not before the year 2030. The actual use of cash, however, can start to become marginal much sooner than that. Sweden is currently in a "tipping point"—a situation where a slow decrease in use of cash has become a rapid decline—and it is likely that this development will continue albeit

---

[1]World Payments Report (2018).

© The Author(s) 2019

N. Arvidsson, *Building a Cashless Society*, SpringerBriefs in Economics,
https://doi.org/10.1007/978-3-030-10689-8_10

with a reduced pace. Another report we made led us to the conclusion that cash may become marginal in 2023 AD.

One critical factor behind the low use of cash in Sweden is that consumers put high trust in the Riksbank as well as the banking and payment system (including its actors) which in combination with a strong technology interest among Swedes has led to a willingness to use electronic payment services rather than cash. Cash is often seen as less convenient than, for instance, cards which are dominating the field of retail payments.

Yet another factor is of course demographics that speak in favor of mobile payment services to the detriment of cash. Younger people prefer electronic payments and are not getting raised with cash in the same sense as previous generations were. It may well be that the future of cash rests with the older generations. Several studies have shown that Swedish consumers in general are reducing their use of cash and this development is likely to continue partly because there is an evident demographic factor behind this pattern. Elderly have a higher tendency to use cash compared to other age groups, and people below 65 are not expected to start using cash to a higher extent just because they turn 65, which means that the use of cash is partly related to demographics. As elderly people using cash today will leave us, the use of cash will decrease.

Another factor is of course all the alternatives to cash that are likely to become more attractive for consumers and therefore become more competitive vis-à-vis cash. A move toward more e- and m-commerce will also speak in favor of more electronic payment services and less cash. Counterarguments, i.e., which may lead to a higher use of cash, include critical failures in the electronic and mobile systems, high fees for electronic and mobile services, a strengthened civil rights movement that convinces politicians and consumers to protect cash from a citizen and consumer perspective, and a general political ambition to keep cash. There are of course many other factors speaking in each direction, but these are some of the most important.

We have also seen that banks are reducing their supply of cash handling services. In 2016 more than half of the banks' retail offices did not provide cash handling services (Länsstyrelserna, 2016). Previous studies also show that while banks may earn significant profits on electronic payment services as card payments, they do not earn much profits on cash-based services (Guiborg & Segendorf, 2007).

Our recent study on merchants' view on cash (Arvidsson, Hedman, & Segendorf, 2018) provides a clear image of a likely development where the last bastion for cash—merchants—progressively stop accepting cash which lead to a situation where the average merchant may not even make profits from cash-based sales in 2023 AD. This is only 5 years from now!

The last decade has shown a continuous decrease in the use of cash in Sweden, and the likely future is that this will continue in the coming years. There is one factor—deteriorating interoperability of cash—that actually may speed up this decline or at least mean that it will not stop. As more and more merchants—probably influenced by each other—say no to cash, more and more consumers are likely to stop using cash, and this circle is likely to make the decline of cash to continue. In addition, other factors like the demographic development and introduction of new innovative services will continue to put pressure on cash and favor electronic and mobile payments. This development is also likely to become favored by the majority of Swedes.

There are of course also factors that work in the opposite direction. We can expect that specific groups in the society—like elderly and people with physical and/or cognitive disabilities—will continue to be dependent on cash and therefore suffer from a reduction of cash. There are also geographical regions where telecommunication systems and Internet access are not reliable and that merchants therefore prefer cash. If these groups are able to make politicians listen to them, we could see a movement that strives to keep cash to help these groups, which then would act to strengthen the position of cash in the Swedish society.

One central conclusion in this book is that the payment system in Sweden faces high degrees of change where a combination of simultaneous change in a number of factors—social, economic, technological, political, and legal—makes it difficult to foresee what may happen in the future. We are currently seeing that contactless cards grow in importance and we can expect the next phase will see growth of mobile payments in stores as well as in m- and e-commerce.

Contactless cards may become the factor that makes merchants to invest in point-of-sales terminals for contactless payments as well as to educate employees and consumers to start paying via mobile devices also in stores. Contactless cards should be understood as transitional objects on the road to contactless payments based on apps in the phones (even if still based on the technological systems for card payments). This will of course also be a way for card operators—e.g., VISA and Mastercard—as well as for large retail banks to continue being dominating players in the payment industry.

Another and more drastic—as well as unpredictable—pattern of change relates to the new regulation in combination with new technologies. The introduction of new legal licenses related to payments in the new payment service directives[2] will enable new actors from Fintech to launch services that compete with banks. We will see more services—some that compete directly with banks' payment services and some that complement them—and more actors. Merchants and consumers are likely to meet lower fees while at the same time facing the challenge to know how to select which service and which service provider to use. Many attempts to revolutionize the payment industry will be made where—as always—some will fail and be forgotten, while others may become the leading firms in an era of a fully digitalized payment system. And, it is likely some of the winners will come from Sweden.

No matter which viewpoint you have regarding the future of cash, you must admit we live in interesting (and either promising or problematic) times when we talk about money and payments!

---

[2]Both PSD1 and PSD2 with the launch of payment institutions, payment initiation service providers, and account information service providers will make it easier to start competing with the traditional banks. It can also be mentioned that other directives like the E-money directive and work aiming to make it easier to switch bank lead in this direction.

References

Arvidsson, N., Hedman, J., & Segendorf, B. (2018). *När slutar svenska handlare acceptera kontanter?* (Handelsrådet, Forskningsrapport 2018:1).

Guiborg, G., & Segendorf, B. (2007). A note on the price- and cost structure of retail payment services in the Swedish banking sector 2002. *Journal of Banking and Finance, 31*, 2817–2827.

Länsstyrelserna. (2016). *Bevakning av grundläggande betalningstjänster 2016.* Falun: Länsstyrelsen i Dalarna.

World Payments Report 2018 by CapGemini and BNP Paribas.